Leonard Clark's bookplate, from a woodcut made for him by Joan Hassall in the early 1960s

EVERY VOICE

LEONARD CLARK

EVERY VOICE
Selected Poems

edited and introduced by
John Howlett

foreword by
Bob Clark

Greenwich Exchange
London

Greenwich Exchange, London

First published in Great Britain in 2024
All rights reserved

Leonard Clark
Every Voice: Selected Poems
© The Literary Executor of Leonard Clark, 2024

Introduction © John Howlett
Foreword © Bob Clark

This book is sold subject to the conditions that it shall not, by way of trade or otherwise, be lent, resold, hired out or otherwise circulated without the publisher's prior consent in any form of binding or cover other than that in which it is published and without a similar condition including this condition being imposed on the subsequent purchaser.

Printed and bound by imprintdigital.com
Cover design by December Publications
Tel: 07951511275

Greenwich Exchange Website: www.greenex.co.uk

Cataloguing in Publication Data is available from the British Library

ISBN: 978-1-910996-84-3

CONTENTS

Bob Clark: Foreword *13*

John Howlett: Introduction *15*

from POEMS (1940)

The Bourgeois *31*

After a Symphony by Glazunov *32*

Conceit *33*

X *34*

In Memoriam: Ivor Gurney *35*

The Moth *36*

from PASSAGE TO THE POLE AND OTHER POEMS (1944)

Journey Between Two Points *37*

Blackbird *39*

Intensity *41*

Scaleber Beck *42*

Victims *43*

Abyss *44*

Exiles *45*

Mystical *46*

from THE MIRROR AND OTHER POEMS (1948)

The Mirror *47*

The Tower *48*

The Lion *49*

The Acorn *50*

The Wilderness *51*

Lamb *52*

Heron *53*

Clamavi *55*

January Morning *56*

The Seeker *57*

Let These Things Be *58*

The Hill *59*

from ENGLISH MORNING AND OTHER POEMS (1953)

The Walk *60*

English Morning *61*

Peace, Like a Lamb *62*

Headlong, Like Comet *63*

The Clock *65*

Invasion *67*

Near Tintern 1798 *68*

Charcoal Burners *69*

Far Headingley *71*

Hedgehog *72*

The Thief *73*

from SELECTED POEMS 1940-1957 (1957)

Village Idiot *74*

The Park *75*

Larks and Curlews *76*

Wild Parsley *77*

from FIELDS AND TERRITORIES (1967)

Bones *78*

The Rocks *79*

Button Box *80*

January *81*

from WALKING WITH TREES (1970)

Samuel Palmer at Shoreham *82*

Expression of Colour *83*

Boy and Grasses *84*

from SECRET AS TOADS (1972)

Assembly of Birds *85*

Bullfinches *86*

Badger *87*

Mushrooms *88*

from SINGING IN THE STREETS (1972)

The Elements *89*

Every Voice *90*

from THE BROAD ATLANTIC (1974)

Peaches *91*

Looking at Cornfields *92*

Bees *93*

Bear *94*

Cave Painting *97*

Grass *99*

Small Life *101*

Hills *102*

Mole *103*

English County *104*

The Pea-Pickers *105*

from **THE HEARING HEART** (1974)
Eyes and Voices *107*
Children of Islington *109*
De La Mare's Bell *110*
In Norfolk *112*
Hedgehog *113*
Fallow *114*

from **SILENCE OF THE MORNING** (1978)
IX 'Working on an old poem late at night ... ' *115*
XIX 'Iron man, speak to me ... ' *116*

from **12 POEMS FROM ST BARTHOLOMEW'S** (1978)
Retreat to Silence *118*

from **THE WAY IT WAS** (1980)
Green Man Wandering *119*
Cider-House *121*
Biological Experiment *123*
Still Born *124*
Maurice *126*
Rector *127*
Sermons in Stones *129*
The Way it Was *131*

from **AN INTIMATE LANDSCAPE** (1981)
I 'A landscape of trees, massed ... ' *132*
III 'Almost no history ... ' *134*

V 'It was the warm smell of honeysuckle ... ' *136*
IX 'It was an orchard of plum trees ... ' *137*
XII 'When the nights drew in, they quietly came back ... ' *139*

Miscellaneous and Uncollected Poems

from WINTER TO WINTER (1979)

XVIII 'I marvel at it ... ' *141*
XIX 'The land, a chessboard of brown squares ... ' *142*

from BURNT SIENA (1980)

The Fortress *143*

Other Poems

When Snow Falls *144*
Silence and Water *145*
Witnesses *146*

Notes
Title Index

FOREWORD

What can a child say about a parent that is relevant in a place like this, other than to express a mix of love, gratitude and regret before moving swiftly on? But I am grateful to Dr John Howlett for giving me the chance to write a few words about my late father, Leonard Clark, as his Literary Executor rather than as his son.

I grew up with the ethos of literary executorship all around me. As a child I was aware of, even if I did not understand, Dad's frustrations with the literary executors of poets whose work he wished to anthologise but who would not answer letters or wanted larger permission fees than the book would support. I observed his struggles as, for a while, he served as a joint literary executor for his great friend Edmund Blunden, as he finally managed to unlock the poetry of Ivor Gurney, and worked in harmony with the literary estates of others such as Walter de la Mare. I learned by osmosis about copyright, permissions, contracts and the like. And then in my teens it dawned on me that one day I too would be a Literary Executor, and that in a very kind and careful way I was being prepared for the task. Then, in the last year of Dad's life, the instructions came – although only in hindsight did I realise what had been happening.

First, I would have to tidy everything up – all the work in progress. Then I had to sort and rationalise everything into a Leonard Clark archive which, Dad was certain, one day someone would come for. Then there was an administrative role that would be with me for my entire life, to protect copyright, handle permissions and gather up what I always knew would be a poet's pittance of income. But above all, my task was to make sure that his work lived on in memory – the mellifluous flow of his stories, the joy and sharing of his poetry for children, and the harder bite of his poems for adults.

With the Leonard Clark archive now safely lodged at Dean Heritage Centre, the local museum for Dad's beloved Forest of Dean, with this new selection of his poems John Howlett has handed me a peach on a plate to encourage a latter-day awareness of Dad's work and to encourage a quickening of interest in a poet who has left us so much of value. It has been a delight to pass on my knowledge and understandings to support John's critical analysis, and both bitter-sweet and enlightening for my sister Mary-Louise and I to revisit our memories and our appreciation of the poet who was our father, and alongside him of our mother Jane who gave him so much inspiration.

I stand with him now in his mind as, at *break of day, in wavering dream (we) heard some fields whispering together.* Do I, too, now look back and see *a green man wandering all his days*?

Bob Clark MA (Oxon), MSc, FMA, FSA Scot
Literary Executor of Leonard Clark
18 May 2024

INTRODUCTION

Few poets of the last century, be they major or minor, have been so inexorably bound to a particular place as Leonard Clark (1905-1981) and the Forest of Dean region of Gloucestershire in which he grew up. Long after he had moved away to London and become part of a literary metropolitan milieu that included close friendships with writers as diverse as Edith Sitwell and John Betjeman, the Forest continued to act as a pervasive theme throughout much of his most important work. Three popular volumes of autobiography, *Green Wood* (1962), *A Fool in the Forest* (1965), and *Grateful Caliban* (1967) rendered lovingly, for example, the characters and incidents of his boyhood – a pre-First World War, quasi-Arcadian rural existence. Likewise, the episodic structure of those memoirs, with each chapter a self-contained story, readily lent themselves for broadcast and thus the mellow rural lilt of Clark's voice could often be heard declaiming passages on the wireless. In a similar vein, a healthy number of Clark's poems, even those composed towards the end of his life, were to derive from his particularly close affinity with landscape and the outdoors, thereby serving as a perpetual reminder of the importance to him of his West Country upbringing.

Today, it is difficult to imagine this remembered world; the old unofficial regional boundaries of the Rivers Wye and Severn have been replaced by the less picturesque pincers of two major motorways (the M4 and the M5) meaning that the historical isolation for so long enjoyed by the Forest and its people has vanished.

A day excursion to the nearby city of Gloucester fifteen miles away – for Clark a rare treat via horse and cart and taking the better part of twenty hours in all – is now a brief morning detour for interested tourists, keen for a glimpse inside its famous cathedral. History too has become heritage with the traditional coal mines, iron works, and steel foundries turned into living museums and artefacts. Even the population, for many years little more than fifty thousand, has seen a recent boom such as to swell the small towns of Cinderford, Lydney and Coleford and, in the process, dilute some of the close family relationships and intricate social dynamics that were so much a part of the world of the young poet.

Aside then from its literary merits – to which we will return – Clark's work, both for adults and children, takes on an additional role in being valuable historical source material and aids us in comprehending a largely vanished time and place, a last outpost of the late Victorian age. Notwithstanding the occasional sentimentalisation of his depictions, and like all good storytellers he was prone to embellishment for dramatic effect, we cannot but doubt either the authenticity of the wide-eyed, Wordsworthian sense of wonder which accompanied his many and varied observations of the natural world, the cycles of which still (just) governed the lives and work of the rural lands in which he was embedded. As he was to later put it, 'I am still that seventeen-year-old boy at heart. I carry around with me such memories as the sunlight on Severn, I can hear the trees talking in Abbotswood, I plough my way, in imagination, through the young snow that, once a year, used to block all the roads from Cinderford to Gloucester ... If I had a drum I would beat it to show how fortunate I am' (Clark, 1965, 157).

Yet, whilst these associations are important to understand and Clark's connection to place never forgotten, two important points of mitigation need to be kept in mind. First, Clark was not a native of the West Country and had in fact been born on Guernsey in the Channel Islands. His mother Louisa had been a servant in London who had fallen pregnant by a well-off diamond merchant. In a country then unsympathetic to children born out of wedlock, she had been sent to a private nursing facility which specialised in such things, to give birth as far away from home as possible. Following money being settled upon his mother, Clark was then moved again to be fostered by a widow (Sarah George) in Cinderford in the Forest of Dean who became a *de facto* parent. He was to later recall how, 'They all came to fetch me, the new baby not much more than a year old, at the little wayside station of Newnham-on-Severn ... I was handed over to Sarah, golden-haired and struggling, tearful from the long journey from London, with my wicker basket of clothes, a letter and the remains of an apple' (Clark, 1962, 31).

This turbulent beginning, the details of which are even today still not clear, meant therefore that Clark remained, to some degree, an adopted son of the region and this, on top of his illegitimacy, perhaps explains why he was constantly striving *to belong*. It seems, after all, a strange fact that for one so in need of the inspiration and succour provided by the trees, fields, and hedgerows of his boyhood surrounds, he was to spend most of his life living and working in cities, notably Leeds and London where he was employed as both a teacher and school inspector. Whilst he was not therefore totally rootless, being for so long twice removed (in both distance and time) from what he saw as his homeland perhaps explains why he could never quite escape the yearning pull of his youth or the sensations it exerted upon his writing.

Second, and once again belying appearances, Clark's voluminous corpus of poetry – of which only about ten percent is reproduced here – did not always conform to the expected patterns of one frequently considered to be a neo-Georgian. Whilst it is true that his earliest work was parochial in its ambitions and weaker by comparison, from *Passage to the Pole* (1944) onwards it was to branch out in unexpected directions. *Pole*, for example, was a darker collection reflecting something of Clark's strained personal situation at the time, whilst *The Mirror* (1948) begun subsequently to exude more obviously visionary qualities, and was reminiscent in its way of those inspirational poets for whom William Blake remained an original point of reference. In form, his later work eschewed strict rhyme and meter and its looser, more relaxed style sat comfortably enough with that of his peers so as to feel contemporary. Although it would be a mistake to characterise Clark as being in any sense a radical – a lifelong High Church man of classical Liberal persuasion is telling enough – it prevails upon us to appreciate him now as a far broader, and better, poet than any cursory reading would suggest.

Whilst Clark's work has therefore the ability (still) to surprise, the key to any real understanding of his corpus lies nevertheless in its highly autobiographical nature with much of his best poetry – typically that about animals, birds, and places – deriving from his own observations and travels. There is little politics in Clark, nor did he attempt to grapple with the wider impacts of urbanization which he saw on an almost daily basis through his visits to schools – 'Children of Islington' is the closest he comes to either of these themes and even this poem is underscored with optimism. More unexpectedly perhaps, he did not attempt seriously to moralise on many of the changes which had overtaken the rural parts of England and that were such an integral part of his own childhood. His poetry was, in many cases, of and about the *self* but not that of the egotistical self; rather, it was self bound to wonder at, and respond to, the natural world – the 'potency of that tuft' ('Grass', line 55) evoking a quasi-pantheist spirit mediated through Clark's orthodox Christian outlook.

That he should however have retained a child-like sense of curiosity around the 'holy mythology' ('Looking at Cornfields', line 3) of nature is, in retrospect, unsurprising. Not only was his childhood a constant wellspring of inspiration to be drawn upon but his working life in education including a 34-year stint as a school inspector (a record to this day!) meant that he was more closely attenuated than most to the curious ways of viewing and understanding the world so characteristic of young people. Despite being in many respects conservatively minded about such matters – he was not wholly opposed to selection into secondary schools and was cautious about the rapid expansion of comprehensives – Clark's career nevertheless intersected with the emergence of child-centred approaches in the state sector, the tenets of which derived from Romantic notions around the innately wise and inquisitive aspects of the child's character. These were principles toward which he was hugely sympathetic and it is worth noting that the best of his children's poetry, represented here by *Secret as Toads* (1972), is barely distinguishable in tone from his adult verse, a fact which seems to suggest that Clark believed in children as able and capable thinkers who should not be spared glimpses into the more savage elements of the world around them: 'And she, hanging dead and alone,/upside down on the spiked wire,/badge streaked with old blood,/torn flesh fermenting round smashed skull' ('Badger', lines 9-12). To that end, Clark was also to play an important role in advising on the teaching of poetry, a subject upon which he expatiated at some length, whilst he also was involved in the organising of training courses on music, drama, and dance.

Such passion for the intrinsic value of the creative arts for the young inevitably drew from his own biography which had seen him begin to write verse from an early age, an endeavour in which he was influenced and encouraged by the local poet and literary celebrity F.W. Harvey who had made his name during the First World War and then became a practicing solicitor: 'I remember him best of all ambling along the country roads, wearing a rather stained navy-blue suit, a battered trilby hat planted firmly on his head, gold-rimmed spectacles on nose, and cigarette between tobacco-stained fingers' (Clark, 1965, 108). Like the budding writer, Harvey too was a loyal son of Gloucestershire, a prolific talker, lover of long walks, and an enthusiastic cricket fan. Their bond was therefore immediate, and such was Harvey's importance to Clark that the latter's first book of poems – the now exceptionally rare *Between the Hills* (1924) – contained several dialect pieces in the style of his mentor as well as a fulsome recommendation as to their merits.

Equally important to Clark at this point, as they had been no doubt to Harvey, were the works of Henry George Nicholls (1825-1867), a local curate who was the first to write seriously on the history of the Forest of Dean. In his three published volumes,

Nicholls had begun to conceive of the Forest as a self-contained, independent entity with its own peculiar sets of customs and mores. Such a view contrasted with earlier accounts that had tended to simply subsume the region within the wider country of Gloucestershire. In a later article entitled 'Free Miners and Foresters' Clark was to speak pointedly of the importance of Nicholls to his own way of thinking: 'I read Nicholls' books in my teens and learned a great deal about my native heath ... How strangely can a few pages of an old book work on one's imagination' (Clark, 1966, 422). In considering Nicholls' influence on Clark, Jason Griffiths rightly tells us that, 'what this rich historical source did [do] was invest Clark's childhood home with a depth of history beyond merely that of his own personal recollections' (Griffiths, 2019, 41).

Time and again within his poetry we observe therefore Clark communing with those elements of the past and attempting to forge and create something distinctive by way of local identity. 'Charcoal Burners' (a favourite of his) for example tells of previous generations of workers in the forest, 'Drawing at upturned pipes or munching bread/As hazel, ash and alder dropped to dust' ('Charcoal Burners', lines 23-24). Elsewhere, and heavily leaning this time on Edmund Blunden, a poem such as 'Maurice' fashions an archetype from one who, 'reads the weather in the country signs' ('Maurice', line 1). As with Wordsworth and the Lake District, John Clare at Helpston and the Fens, Samuel Palmer at Shoreham, and even Stanley Spencer in Cookham, Clark was profoundly connected to his own sense of place. It was what he thought with and the pull it exerted was relentless: 'I breathe some of its divinity now,/am washed by it as these hills are washed,/know that Love is shining here, everlasting' ('An English County', lines 21-23). Even when not drawing from it explicitly, its *genius loci* imbued the spirit and sense of much of his poetry.

Making something fresh of the landscape in this way, however, required experience and this explains why it took Clark time to mature and establish himself as an original creative force. He was anyway no meteor – he referred jokingly to his neophyte self as being an 'innocent abroad, versifying' – and well into his thirties what poetry he did manage to publish in newspapers and magazines was juvenilia and not later collected into book form. Even after his initial move to London in 1930 to take up his first full-time teaching post – for which incidentally Harvey never forgave him! – and his introduction to those in the literary sets of Soho and Fitzrovia, Clark's voice continued to remain derivative. Despite being taken on eventually by a major publisher, his first 'proper' book of verses, *Poems* (1940), was similarly somewhat imitative, most obviously of Walter de la Mare whose work Clark had come to revere. In time de la Mare was to become a close friend and inspire the evocative 'de la Mare's Bell'. However, such influences were at this stage too obviously betrayed, and it is no coincidence that the most successful works in *Poems* are a handful of proto-Imagist pieces and satires, far removed from his prevailing West Country, Georgian roots.

The catalyst therefore for Clark's emergence as a poet of note and with a voice to call his own was his transfer to the West Riding in January 1943, an appointment which followed six and a half years as an Assistant Inspector in Plymouth, Devon. Although his inspectorial memoir dwells little on his personal life, preferring instead to concentrate on events within the educational sphere in which he worked, there is nonetheless a clear acknowledgement that his time spent in Yorkshire was crucial to his development as a writer. In part however this change *was* rooted in the personal; the previous years had seen Clark lose a young son to illness, an event which led to his wife deserting him and a subsequent period of depression. The poems which followed, many sporting such titles as 'Terror', 'Abyss', 'Victims' and 'Checkmate Every Move', reflected his turbulent circumstances and were later to form the backbone of *Passage to the Pole* (1944), Clark's bleakest and most obviously autobiographical collection in which his own anger and distress was palpable. This was poetry as catharsis and, feeling himself a 'mateless eagle ... knowing the meaning of a cheated spring' ('Abyss', lines 16 and 18), he was to request a transfer in an attempt to move as far away as possible from the south coast and the raw associations it still carried.

Abstaining himself from this difficult personal situation is however only a partial explanation for the arrival of Clark, the fully-formed poet. For the rest we need only look to the social and cultural circles in which his new post allowed him to circulate. Lodging in Leeds with the composer Edward Allam meant Clark became acquainted with such luminaries as Christopher Hassall (with whom he collaborated on a short-lived literary press) and Imogen Holst, but also academics within a range of fields from the nearby university. Equally significant, he was also appointed as the reviewer of poetry for *The Yorkshire Post* which meant that he came into regular contact with genres and styles of writing to which he may previously have been unaware or unsympathetic. Anything and everything now passed under Clark's nose including not only poets of the front rank such as Sitwell and Betjeman but also those destined to be undeservedly (John Lehmann) as well as legitimately (Wilfrid Rowland Childe) forgotten.

As a reviewer Clark was scrupulous but likewise fair and open-minded and this receptivity to new writing was to impact on his own work in a palpable way. One such experiment was a long poem entitled *Rhandanim* which he was later to describe as a 'mad and rather fantastic effort in my best apocalyptic style, full of sound and fury, glorious technicolour and fake orientalism. It was the kind of thing that Coleridge might have tossed off after a couple of doses of laudanum' (Clark, 1976, 95). This later assessment is accurate and passages such as, 'And on an ivory nail is hung/a cabinet of speaking bells,/whose turrets quaked in Turkestan,/and spilled in blue Byzantium/their ripples on the dove-thick air' ('Rhandanim', lines 98-102) border on pastiche and Clark is perhaps to be thanked for having had no desire to later reprint this long and somewhat chaotic affair. Nonetheless, this failure was atypical and other verse produced in the Leeds years was able to channel this new spirit more successfully. Take for example, 'Blackbird' which has the dream-like and dislocating quality of a landscape by Paul Nash: 'He skimmed over the hedge/In orange and black/And saw in the field by the willow tree wood/Two skulls which he knew/Were the end of his quest' ('Blackbird', lines 1-5). Equally adeptly drawn were 'Lamb' stretching its 'rigid shanks/In wondering measurement' ('Lamb', line 7) and 'Heron' – memorably 'Postured to a question-mark' ('Heron', line 6) – whose very means of survival is rendered in the most graphic of terms: 'Bearing aloft upon his dripping spear/The doomed and gaping trout/Whose torn gills beat in tides of agony' (Ibid, lines 29-31). It would not be stretching a point to claim these images as acting as a forerunner by almost a decade to the work of Ted Hughes, another destined to become a close friend of Clark. Although Hughes' poetry was to develop a broader philosophy, often by drawing upon folklore and emphasizing the malevolent and nurturing aspects of nature, both writers nonetheless shared a keen awareness of the potent and sometimes irrational energies found within animal life. It is no surprise that Clark was to review favourably Hughes' first two volumes ('Watch this poet, if he continues to write poetry and develop at the present rate, he has a glowing future') or that Hughes was to hold Clark in such high regard as a pioneer in capturing the raw and unfiltered qualities of landscape.

This divinatory and shamanic tone, so later admired, pervaded Clark's own volume *The Mirror*, published in 1948 and his first properly original collection, with several of the book's early poems such as the title piece, 'The Tower', 'The Lion', and 'The Wilderness' situating the reader in parched, quasi-Biblical landscapes populated by mythical beasts and the bedraggled remnants of humanity. The description of a 'great tower of skulls/Stretching from earth to heaven' ('The Tower', lines 1-2) is especially memorable and is an easy bedfellow to comparable poems by John Jarmain and Paul Dehn, both of whom used similarly arid imagery (the skull, bones, decay) to offer comment on the ravages of the Second World War. Although this was a world unknown to Clark – he served briefly and by his own admission ineffectually in the Home Guard – it is nonetheless worth noting that he was to later dedicate 'The Thief' to Henry Treece, a leading light with J.F. Hendry of the short-lived New Apocalyptic school whose stock in trade was similarly nightmareish metaphors and the primacy of myth. In Clark's case, the myths were Christian and he was to draw upon its various elements to offer suggestive comment on broader post-War uncertainty and trauma: 'And then I hammered nails/Into the shrieking trees,/And on my face I felt their blood/And on their cheeks, my tears' ('The Seeker', lines 13-16).

Whilst his faith was to remain and strengthen over time, he was not to deploy it in this way again and, as the small post-war cliques and factions became subsumed under the broader umbrella of neo-romanticism, so did Clark also move with the times; 'The Walk' and 'Headlong, Like Comet', for example, drew clearly from Dylan Thomas and inhabit similar territory to that previously colonised by 'Fern Hill'. The resemblance is not only visual – long, overflowing lines mimicking the wandering of distant memory and the recollection of the past in small chunks – but also in the luscious abundance of imagery and symbolism; plums as 'cascades of rubies' and ferns waving 'spidered in sunlight' serve as evocative invocations of the state and sensation of childhood. Inevitably perhaps Clark's work lacks the advanced half- and internal rhymes of Thomas, nor does he seek to personify Time as a guardian who was to hold the young child 'green and dying'. This however works in Clark's favour; whereas Thomas preferred to see childhood as a bout of mercy before the trials of adulthood, there is no such reservation in 'Headlong' which ends in a passage of contentment: 'So I watched in my wonder till stars pricked the heavens and I/walked in the coolness/To the ease of the farmhouse through the dew and the grasses' ('Headlong, Like Comet', lines 34-36).

It is however important not to go too far in over-emphasizing the experimentalism within Clark. Although it is true that his time in Leeds and subsequent reviewing had urged him into contemporaneity, and the best of his later work was, after that fashion, to incorporate a looser and more relaxed style often eschewing capital letters and regular rhyme schemes, it nevertheless rarely strayed far from a central set of concerns and preoccupations. A case in point is 'The Pea-Pickers', one of his best poems, and which cannot but be compared to 'The Whitsun Weddings' both in its subject matter (a train journey through Lincolnshire) but also its Larkinesque opening: 'Travelling north, a glazed afternoon in June, the train slowed down, and stopped' ('The Pea-Pickers', lines 1-2). However, whereas Larkin's eye, with characteristic pessimism, was moved to understand observed social behaviours (urban) in the context of a wider sense of impermanence of both life and joy, Clark's subjects (rural) were more defined by their stoicism. The lives of the agricultural labourers – straight from the brush of Clausen – were seen as regulated by nature's unchanging cycle: 'patiently moving forward, baskets crammed,/the self-same rhythm, season after season,/life, death, and resurrection' ('The Pea-Pickers', lines 29-31). These were men and women held in aspic, and, to his credit, Clark was never seriously to tackle contemporary subjects. Indeed, in his poetic tributes to fellow poets Hardy and Andrew Young (the subject of 'Green Man Wandering'), as well as the artist Samuel Palmer, Clark can be seen as appropriating himself into a particular thread of Englishness – what may best be termed a reasoned pastoral – and it was from this turf that much of his best writing was to germinate.

Ultimately, Clark's was a poetry in which, at its best, nothing was invented. His poems were, rather, born of *experience* and were outgrowths of an acute sensitivity to the world he knew, one which could be described by the most exquisite of sounds: 'a waterfall of wings' ('Peace, Like a Lamb', line 14) disturbing a reverie to take one striking example. On occasion, Clark's experiences also lead him to moments of great poignancy – 'Still Born' for instance, drawn from his own recollections of losing a child, is used even now by support groups. The last line, as so often in these poems ('Death and life are the same mysteries'), carries the heft. Elsewhere, particularly amongst his later poems, we find too moods of recollection, although he rarely fell into the easy trap of yearning for a long-departed way of life. Instead, the prevailing feeling is one of resigned acceptance as in 'Cider-House' which refuses to condemn the displacement of older traditions at the expense of mechanisation and with the poem ending in a moment of characteristic reflection: 'I say each one to myself now, lovely on my tongue,/as ripe and rounded as cider itself,/drunk with long memories from a china mug' ('Cider-House', lines 39-41).

We should of course be alive to the weaknesses within Clark and acknowledge that he is probably best read in selection. As an instinctive and therefore prolific poet with nearly five hundred poems to his name as well as a large number still unpublished, variations in quality are inevitable and when stepping outside of his hinterland such as those poems about America (a place he never visited and with knowledge derived from acquaintances) in *The Broad Atlantic* (1975) the results are perhaps less convincing. Similarly, his religious work such as those verses making up the bulk of *Singing in the Streets* (1972) (all of which were sent as family Christmas cards) and *Silence of the Morning* (1978) are more workmanlike and bloodless affairs, have clear designs on the reader, and do not challenge the view that the last fifty years have produced few poems of the first rank on these themes. There is also a sense that his epithets and description occasionally verge on the mundane; 'shy anemones', 'murmuring water', and 'lovely wood' (all taken from *English Morning*) are old hat.

That being said, to read the best of Clark, whatever that hackneyed phrase might mean, is to keep company with a poet of integrity, honesty, and an uncompromising simplicity in how he presents the world around him and his own feelings towards it. It is also to become familiar with poems which, to paraphrase Robert Frost, so often begin in delight and end in wisdom and it is the wisdom of one who had a deep and sympathetic understanding of the subjects about which he wrote. These are violets beside mossy stones and he shares much with those who had influenced and shaped his writing – in particular Harvey, de la Mare, and Andrew Young. Appraising the latter's poetry, Clark was to make the point that, '[Young's] work ... is still not as well known as it should be. It has never been taken up, even with sober enthusiasm, by any clique. The most retiring of men ... He has no disciples, for he is no prophet, though there are many who envy his skill with words and his good common sense. He is certainly in no danger of ever becoming a literary fashion' (Clark, 1957, 11). This was a telling observation for it could equally apply to Clark's own body of work which, despite its successful assimilation of wider influences, tended always to stand to one side of the major schools and currents of the century, be they Modernism, the Movement, or neo-Romanticism. Poems written as late as the 1960s and 1970s disguised their temporal origins and, in their subject matter, harked back to the pre-occupations of the Georgians. John Betjeman was therefore right to assert how, 'He [Clark] refused to court popularity by resorting to gimmickry ... he remained constant to his ideals and to his self-imposed standard' (Betjeman,1984, n.p.).

One consequence of this steadfastness has been that fewer readers today are acquainted with Clark with even his anthology pieces having fallen from favour. Tellingly, he does not merit a mention in either the *Dictionary of National Biography* or major anthologies of the century such as those by Ian Hamilton (1996) or Keith Tuma (2001). What little scholarship exists has tended to focus on his work for children which, whilst important, is a significant lacuna when considering the enormous range of Clark's wider output – not just the poetry but anthologies, critical studies, autobiographies, and books on teaching. Such collective amnesia has not been helped either by the lack of a complete archive or record of Clark's papers, many of which (often the letters from illustrious correspondents) were sold by him in the 1960s.[1]

However, whilst these facts remain pertinent, they should in no way serve to denigrate the quality of the poems contained within your hands which represent, in the judgement of the current author, a good representation not only of the many facets of their subject

---

[1]This situation has now been rectified with the Clark archive being stored at the Dean Heritage Centre. I am indebted here to Bob Clark, Leonard's son, who allowed me early access to the letters, drafts, unpublished poems, and ephemera which have remained in the family.

but also his trajectory across the years. They should also disabuse us of any residual feeling that Clark was only known and appreciated by a narrow group of contemporaries. Lest it be forgotten that his poetry sold well amongst the general public, and he was honoured by the Establishment in his election as a Fellow of the Royal Society of Literature in 1953 and the award of an OBE in 1966. More revealingly the publication of *A Garland of Poems*, a festschrift for his 75th birthday, contained pieces from poets as disparate as R.S. Thomas, Peter Redgrove, Kathleen Raine, and David Gascoyne, many of whom had over time become his friends and grown to respect his achievement. That Clark could attract such admiration says much not just for the worth of his poetry – his reputation grew with his bibliography – but also his fundamentally decent character and tireless efforts in promoting the value of literature for those of all ages and backgrounds. His more scholarly work convinced us too of the permanent value of Ivor Gurney and Alfred Williams whilst he devoted much time to giving talks and readings around the country. His belief in the importance of public service was enacted through membership of numerous committees including being Consultant on Poetry for the Seafarers' Education Service (1940-1954) and on the Literature Panel of the Arts Council (1965-1969)

Prolific to the end, and shortly after a last visit to the Forest where he was acclaimed for his contributions, Clark died the following year, 10 September 1981. In accordance with his wishes, half of his ashes were scattered from Symonds Yat, a beauty spot straddling the River Wye, whilst the other half were interred in St Stephen's Church, Cinderford where he had long ago been the organist. This last rite reunited fittingly the two key threads which had been woven through so much of his life and work – landscape and boyhood. A green man, finally, at rest.

John Howlett
July 2024

THE BOURGEOIS

AUTUMN, the murderer,
has throttled the life out of summer
and opened ripe arteries
with a knife wind.
Now in a cloak of fog
he stalks the roads at dawn
wiping bloody fingers
on cowering hedges
and gibbering to the birdless skies.

from POEMS (1940)

AFTER A SYMPHONY BY GLAZUNOV

THERE roll Ukrainian fields,
amber tides of heavy wheat
flowing in rich glory to the morning sun
brave as laughing Cossacks.
What deep repose is here
in these peasant meadows
acres shining with uncut promise!
The blue and distant hills
see old Pushkin smiling on the plain.

from POEMS (1940)

CONCEIT

THAT day the spring
brought crying lambs
and breaking buds and leaping things;
the hedgerow banks were citadels
of primrose built.
And you were set
in innocence
amid it all,
dark hair, ripe curve,
amid it all.
And I became a leaping thing,
a bud, a hedgerow waterfall,
and in me bloomed the flower of you,
the suddenness
of primrose there.

from POEMS (1940)

X

STRANGE woman,
coiled in the wicker chair
beneath the yellow light
with legs criss-crossed in silk and shadow,
you do not see
the watchspring of my mind
poised delicately
pulsing its beat.
I think my thoughts
behind a mask
Gioconda born.
How insecure you are
for all your arrogance.

from POEMS (1940)

IN MEMORIAM: IVOR GURNEY
OBIT 26 xii 37

THESE Severn meadows knew
He would not come
To tread their little paths again.
A whisper, secret as the dew,
Fell from the trembling lips of men,
'An English singer's dumb'
But still the river glides his madrigals
Their cadences of richest Tudor sound:
In Framilode, a winter blackbird calls
Daffodils from frozen ground,
And Gloucester tower,
That certainty of stone and power,
Has heard once more
His timeless music soar,
His young heart rise,
Triumphantly to Cotswold skies.

from POEMS (1940)

THE MOTH

I CANNOT escape from this room.
It mocks me, and the breath
from rotting flowers make it a tomb
wherein breeds death.
Cold lie the fire's embers too;
pictures on the walls leer
and grimace challengingly in imprisoned falsehood.

There flits from the night, a moth, circling near
the flame
of my dwindling candle as to woo
its lover with a final kiss of blood ...

The shrivelled frame
in one embrace has tasted sweetness of eternity.

But where's escape for me?

from POEMS (1940)

JOURNEY BETWEEN TWO POINTS

ALL of a piece now,
The light and the time,
The shadow on wall;
For purpose will out.
The door opened its arms
And welcomed him in,
That stranger of doom
With the smile and the word,
And the warmth left the fire.
The sword which he took
Found its sheath in a heart
No surgeon can patch,
No miracle, heal.
And the room where he stood
On that far-scattered night
With the spring at the turn,
(The years knew the plan
Of the pattern to be)
Has at length found a voice
That was dumb with its hurt,
And cries to the heart,
Now emptied and drained,
That all is a piece
And purpose will out.

Like a tick in the brain,
Purpose will out

Tick in the brain,
Purpose
Will
Out;
Tick ...

from PASSAGE TO THE POLE AND OTHER POEMS (1944)

BLACKBIRD

HE skimmed over the hedge
In orange and black,
And saw in the field by the willow tree wood
Two skulls which he knew
Were the end of his quest.
And he stood
In that Golgotha place
Where no violets nor primroses grew;
And the tangling sedge
Imprisoned his feet
And brought him to rest
In the teeth of the track.
White-pillowed, wind-washed to the bone,
Jowl-rocking and empty of face,
Sang the skulls by the side
Of a weed-rotten pool,
Not knowing each other in death.
Sang the skulls in the comb of the wind
Their echoless rote,
Their meaningless airs.
And he stared out of eyes
Set hard in their stone
At horizonless skies
And remembered retreat,
And the hour when his breath
As eager as theirs
Had once in *him* died,
And mocked him for fool,

Throttled and pinned
The song in his throat,
Maimed his wing beat,
Twisted his note.

from PASSAGE TO THE POLE AND OTHER POEMS (1944)

INTENSITY

DESOLATE
I climb mind spirals,
Treading
Round and round
Unendingly.

A squirrel in a cage,
A rat on a treadmill,
Have less frustration.

Yet a thorn hedge is beautiful
When the archangel
Stretches
His sword.

from PASSAGE TO THE POLE AND OTHER POEMS (1944)

SCALEBER BECK

BREAK, then, this heart,
In the predestined place
Where river and rock
Will remember no face,
Nor tangle of weeds
Give back the shock
And the limb-blunted sound
Of new death
When black waters part.
Finger no beads;
This is old burial ground.
Ghost echoes of sudden stopped breath
Are emptied on limitless air
And dissolved in a dream
Of owl-dimming light,
Never more bruised upon stone.
Stifle the prayer;
Let the tongues of the stream
Here cleft in their pain,
Run mute in the night,
And the bird that sits grieving alone
Be silent again.

from PASSAGE TO THE POLE AND OTHER POEMS (1944)

VICTIMS

TO final ash
there break
roots of tortured trees.
Racked boughs no longer feel
the inquisition lash
from sudden forest flames
which now their members seize.
Trees have lost their names
and found the martyrs' stake.
Not one charred bloodless leaf
can breathe a single prayer
nor lift a voice to make
a gesture of appeal
a pleading for relief
upon the burning air.

from PASSAGE TO THE POLE AND OTHER POEMS (1944)

ABYSS

YET once this sapless tree had iron root,
And octopus it clung to granite rock
With all the vigour of a sapling shoot,
Until it snapped before the shock
Of many winds upon its budding face,
And crashed in ruin down the precipice.
It could not find within itself
Sufficient strength with which to brace
Its quivering limbs upon that naked shelf,
Though every blast had called an armistice;
And so it withered in a dead ravine.
And there its bruised and still-born leaves
Now turn poor broken eyes to where
Marooned in space
And dragging heavy wing,
A mateless eagle grieves
In awful isolation of suspended air;
And both commune and know the meaning of a cheated spring.

from PASSAGE TO THE POLE AND OTHER POEMS (1944)

EXILES
D.J.C.

AND one shall then return,
Though two shall strangely come
Upon the morning tide.

And one shall stay and learn
In grief's millennium,
What are the fruits of pride.

And one shall storm the wave
To seek another light
Beyond the looming reef.

And one shall find a grave,
And there marooned in night
Strike seams of new belief.

from PASSAGE TO THE POLE AND OTHER POEMS (1944)

MYSTICAL

NEITHER Plato, nor Galileo,
who worshipped truth,
could have discovered the meaning behind
the eye of firecrest or oriole.

And Paracelsus,
for all his juggling with stars,
must have started back confounded
at the mystery which huddled
in the whitethroat's nest.

Loyola split ethical hairs
but held God in his hand
when he balanced on wondering palm
the hatching egg of warbler.

from PASSAGE TO THE POLE AND OTHER POEMS (1944)

THE MIRROR

I HELD a mirror in my hand
Wherein I saw with nightmare eyes
The end of Time and Prophecy.
The sea was there, delivered up to fire,
So terrified it could not loose its dead,
The wild beasts were abroad
And ran about the land with devilish mouths;
I could not take my darling from the lions.
Upon a quaking tower the blackened Gabriel stood
And could not blow upon his buckled horn,
And in a burning garden wept the Son of Man
Over His New Jerusalem.

from THE MIRROR AND OTHER POEMS (1948)

THE TOWER

I SAW a great tower of skulls
Stretching from earth to heaven
And growing whiter in air.
And at its base were other bones, marrowless,
And abandoned in loose tumbling piles;
And with them children played.
And widows with grief-lidded eyes
Silently searched among them.
So high this tower its apex pierced the sky,
Then toppled down upon the floors of Paradise
A million jaws
Which made their pitiful speech
To all the innocent spirits there.

from THE MIRROR AND OTHER POEMS (1948)

THE LION

HE comes suddenly into the peopled places,
A lion out of Judah,
With terrible visage and breath,
A voice like waterfalls.

He pierces with dread eye the rocky places
And dark vegetation,
He advances when scenting his prey
To the world's edge and beyond it.

He roars hungrily in the broken places,
That lion out of Judah,
Choosing white lambs on the hills,
Not to ravish but to woo them.

from THE MIRROR AND OTHER POEMS (1948)

THE ACORN

HOLDING an acorn in my hand
I saw the tree that from its heart
Should rise and fall.
Then armies of trees
Marching in triumph over captured hills,
Drummed by the wind,
To make a century's assault upon
The slow-retreating plain.
And then far down the ranks of forests gone to war
I heard the conquering axes ring,
And mourning birds,
An armistice of silence in shattered avenues,
And last, the groan of keels
That moved into the nameless regions of the neutral sea.

from THE MIRROR AND OTHER POEMS (1948)

THE WILDERNESS

HE dwelt among scorpions,
Was wounded by briars,
Out of holes came the lions
Their eyes hot as fires,
Watched Him by starlight,
Sought other prey;
The owls saw Him there
And then sagged away
Into limitless night.
The dew in His hair,
He wandered alone,
His pillow, a stone.
And at the dawn,
The dark crucified,
The last star withdrawn,
There flowed from the side
Of some jutting rock,
Split by the spears
Of lightning's steel shock
Water and tears.
The thorn gave a sigh
And sweated its trails;
Deep stabbing the sky,
Five birds like five nails.
He wandered alone
Where darkness slow bled,
Its ending unknown,
The day broke, blood red.

from THE MIRROR AND OTHER POEMS (1948)

LAMB

FASHIONED in the secret dark
In the dead days of the year
When earth and sky were stark,
Each bud, a mutineer
Within the breaking ranks
Of winter's regiment,
You stretch your rigid shanks
In wondering measurement
And test the spring-charged air.
And as the snow slips from the pines
In tiny thunderings, where
The woods are starred with celandines,
About the garden world you leap
The first of all the paschal sheep.

from THE MIRROR AND OTHER POEMS (1948)

HERON

SOLITARY in ruffled water,
Bill and legs mirrored yellow upon the lapping river,
The old heron waits
Deep to the knees
Above the bough-entangled weir
Postured to a question-mark.
The last faint evening noises meet the oncoming stars
As gorgon-wise he bends his crested head
Whiter than marble or the tufted thistledown
Over the fringing rushes.
And on an island anchored in the darkening stream
His second brood of naked fledglings pierce
The drowsing air with eager cries
Where hollow ruins merge themselves with night,
And every outline, every tree is blurred.
His thoughts and jewelled eyes are not on these
But centred on each growing ring that now and then
Fingers the fading ripples with lightest pencil tracery.
There in a moving world of peopled weed,
Half light, half sound,
Fish scurry from hole to hole,
Blind to the fatal sword that points its threatening stretch
Above their flashing voyagings.
And then,
As shriller come the pipings
From the careless architecture of the heronry,
He stabs the surface with a dagger lunge
And rises clumsily over the shallows and fields
Bearing aloft upon his dripping spear

The doomed and gaping trout
Whose torn gills beat in tides of agony,
Whose dulled eyes catch the streaks of final light,
As higher still he mounts on rounded wing
Spanning the moonlit regions in undivided majesty.

from THE MIRROR AND OTHER POEMS (1948)

CLAMAVI

I HELD His hands in water
And the cool stream ran between our fingers;
He moved His head towards me in the darkness
And kissed my cheek.
I could not see the sadness in those eyes
But felt a tear run down my bended neck.
And heard it meet the waiting water.
O, all the sorrow of the world was in that single tear,
And all acceptance in His kiss;
Love flowed between the lockings of our hands
And soothed the restless water.
No other tide shall rise like this
Nor come a fuller flood of understanding
But I shall feel again that clasp, that kiss,
And know the troubled stream is charged with fire,
And I renewed.

from THE MIRROR AND OTHER POEMS (1948)

JANUARY MORNING

LET all cease now,
Silence be a surgeon to the wounded air,
Snow straighten the cracked bough,
Clothe every stone that is bare,
Reshape the abandoned plough,
Whiten field-fare.

Let the wind speak
No whirling argument of biting word,
But fall to quiet, and seek
Places where sound is interred,
Fill with song the brave cheek
Of storm-mocking bird.

from THE MIRROR AND OTHER POEMS (1948)

THE SEEKER

I WENT into the wood at beetle dusk
Moving like a ghost through wet ferns and grasses,
Seeking in this graveyard of old dead thoughts
Some tokens of remembrance.
No bird sang, and no leaves stirred
And the flowers were white with weariness,
As the moths came out of silent pools, one by one,
Into the eye of the waking moon;
But in this place there was no grief.
And so I twined about my head
The pale stems of bryony
And round my neck an ivy wreath;
And then I hammered nails
Into the shrieking trees,
And on my face I felt their blood
And on their cheeks, my tears.

from THE MIRROR AND OTHER POEMS (1948)

LET THESE THINGS BE

FROM the forgotten grave comes no memory's ghost
To slide unwanted into the cold mind,
Nor from dead days a challenging host
Of old sounds to leave bitter echoes behind.

Remembrance of sad things is sharper than a wound
Made to smart more when dabbed with vinegar,
It is the hope for shape when a branch is pruned,
It is praise to the knife for the gift of a scar.

It is like the washing away of footprints in sand
Made by drowned lovers on a well-known shore,
When nothing remains but the wet land,
And the whine of the gulls and the sea's roar.

Let these things be, buried in mountains of dust,
Let them remain unsifted until the rocks of the earth
Break faith with each other, and the first gust
From a new-blowing wind call them all to rebirth.

from THE MIRROR AND OTHER POEMS (1948)

THE HILL

THE hill of scattered feathers
Floats over shorn meadows below,
Where in disordered lines the shocks
Stagger like a pillaging army
Round tractor and barn,
Over the curves of the land
And so out of sight.

Now in the tangled marsh
The fatal sundew winks a disappearing eye
At wandering insects
In the dissipated light,
Who hear not warning click of grasshopper
Snapping with scissor blade
Near warm sliced rock.

And in the fireflied night
The plover stifles his complaint,
And from the angled branches of some barren tree
The white owl with his face in fog
Strains curious eyes to pierce the empty gloom,
While on the topmost fell
The shepherd leans his crook against a thorn
And tells his sheep by candlelight.

from THE MIRROR AND OTHER POEMS (1948)

THE WALK

for Edmund Blunden

WHEN, head high in corn, I walked with my mother the long,
   golden meadows,
Light on my feet, and sailor-bloused, the whole wide world of
   summer,
She saw beyond, the dark and looming forest
Deep with its undergrowth waiting to seize all travellers,
But I the easy mouse, happily swaying on ripe wheat-stalks
   bending
Over the tangled straw-lanes, trodden and wandering among first
   shadows.
My eyes were all shining and open, my ears quick to the nibbling,
But she held my hand tightly, and the touch of her satin
Was lovely and cool to my fingers, her warmth to my wondering
As her watch ticked away and I heard her heart beating,
Till we passed through the stone stile by broken-down barley
And came to the farmhouse where the big, lumbering horses
Were drinking spring water, mouths foam-flecked from harvest.
Secure in the paddock beneath doves round the windows
She suddenly smiled as she looked at my wide eyes
And smoothed down my wild hair in the starred light of evening.

from ENGLISH MORNING AND OTHER POEMS (1953)

ENGLISH MORNING

    for Christopher Hassall

A LARK is singing in the sky
And over the dreaming fields,
And over the hedges, crowned with may,
Loud with the noise of raiding bees.
All else sleeps on;
Cold in his form the hare awaits
To hear the cock's first bugle note.
Poised like a fluttering star,
The lark beneath him sees
The acres curve their shapes across the countryside,
And when he drops to earth, far off he hears
The cock at last ring out his stuttering call;
And then the hare pricks back his ears
As from the smoking cottages
The yawning farmer comes to stump along the lane,
And squeezing through each squat stone stile
Nods to his ploughman, caught in sun and mist,
And whistling to the drowsy horses and the sky.
A butterfly, new born, tries in the air
His first unsteady flight,
And all along the shining hills
The mushrooms heave themselves to dewy life,
The mole retreats, the squabbling geese march out
To storm the morning with their angry cries.

from ENGLISH MORNING AND OTHER POEMS (1953)

PEACE, LIKE A LAMB

I LIE sleepless in the half light,
Seeing through bare trees outside
The grey wolf sky of pallid stars.
I lie alone and wait,
Not for the tap of robin's beak upon the pane,
The unexpected wind that shakes
The icicles along the eaves
And ruffles up the new-dropped snow,
I wait for every earthly sound to die away;
Until from nothingness I slowly hear
Peace, like a lamb, move soft from field to field,
The crunching tread of strangers on the hills,
And unfamiliar voices in the trees,
And then, a waterfall of wings
Taking possession of the startled air.

from ENGLISH MORNING AND OTHER POEMS (1953)

HEADLONG, LIKE COMET
for Percy Wilson

THERE was a day when, the forest behind, and the waters of Severn
Bright shining and curling before me through buttercupped meadows,
I raced, in the flush of my childhood, from the top of a hill, madly on turf,
Down through the fern on the slope, waving in soft, spidered sunlight,
Wild through the air and into the sky of my seeking, scattering the sheep where they quietly grazed
Near hedges, dark-foaming with nightshade and woodbine, and death mask of foxglove,
Headlong like comet, with the fire and force of my charging, I left cottage and paddock
To dream in their sleep, while the heavy-eyed sow and the cock on a gate
Watched me rush over molehill and hummock, arms like a bird, winged high in my joy,
Out of light into shadow, shade into sun, one leap over water-cressed stream
And then into orchards of white-aproned women shaking the boughs of fat trees
And plums falling down to the earth, cascades of rubies, soundless through air
Into baskets and barrels wide open-mouthed, while old men in braces and patches
Picked up the jewels with warm hands, brown in the morning, and touched all their ripeness
In sight of the soft fussing fowls and ladders criss-crossing in leaves.

They looked at my eyes when I stopped like a stone from a sling,
    for I saw through the trees to the hills,
A boat on the river, squat towers of the churches, fields curving
    and fallow,
And out-topping hedges, wide acres of barley, ten centuries of
    peace, ten centuries of stone;
So I watched in my wonder till stars pricked the heavens and I
    walked in the coolness
To the ease of the farmhouse through the dew and the grasses.

from ENGLISH MORNING AND OTHER POEMS (1953)

THE CLOCK
for Iris

MADE by John Boyce of Dereham in the year
When first Big Ben chimed out at Westminster,
This clock, a monument to his dead skill,
Tick tocks away its speeding memories.
Boyce thought, the simple craftsman that he was,
To cram all time within one figured case;
With certainty he crowned the Roman hours
With man-in-moon, and smiling god-in-sun
Set in a double sky of clouds and stars,
And like another Prospero displayed
An island with a battered ship at sea,
Sails lit by antique lanterns at the helm.
He viewed chronology with dusty eye
Forgetting, as each second knocked away,
That time too soon became eternity;
For see, the roses fade on lacquered face,
The sun and moon stand still as once they did
In Joshua's warring wilderness,
The stars have long since set, the straining ship
Can never reach her longed-for harbour now;
The patient worm is working in the wood.
And yet, this steady enginry recalls
A century or more of births and deaths,
The changing kings and queens upon the wall,
The ghosts of half a dozen sleeping cats,
And grandfather on slippered Sunday nights
Put down his Martin Tupper with a sigh,
And with determined turn of grating key
Start up an eight-day week on wheels again.
But when the old man died, the clock
Gave slowly in to fluff and verdigris,

And said the time was always half past three
For nearly twenty lying years until,
Restored to life it tells the truth again
And strikes the nodding silence of the air
And challenges the startled calendar.

from ENGLISH MORNING AND OTHER POEMS (1953)

INVASION

HAREBELLS ambushed in the grasses
Watch each butterfly that passes
Overhead in dewy light,
And at starry dead of night
Hear the reconnoitring moths
Floating by like plundering Goths.
And at dawn the iron flies
Storm with all their thousand eyes
At the peaceful harebell shade,
While intent on sudden raid
Wide the spider throws his net
And the wasp with bayonet
Stabs all comers flying there,
Trespassers in that blue air.

from ENGLISH MORNING AND OTHER POEMS (1953)

NEAR TINTERN 1798

WORDSWORTH sat here with silent Dorothy
Watching the salmon leap through bubbled air,
The silver water wimpling by,
The gargoyle faces of the rocks;
But all the peace of murmuring Wye,
The shepherds leading out their flocks
From dewy folds and sleeping farms,
Could not allay their deep despair.
For she held Coleridge in her arms,
Half-drugged, at sunny Alfoxden,
And he tramped streets with wild Annette,
Where heads of king and citizen
Whirled round on lifted bayonet.
But as the rowanberries dropped their blood
Upon the slowly-darkening stream,
They moved through woods of sycamore
Green-lit with eyes and hellebore,
To where, as in a waking dream,
They saw the moon in harvest flood,
And on a new, transcended shore,
The arch of Tintern riding high
The cloudy forests of the sky.

from ENGLISH MORNING AND OTHER POEMS (1953)

CHARCOAL BURNERS

IN a dark wood that once I knew
There is a ring scored in the ground
Whose charred face stares on sullen skies
And near a well that bubbles into fern
Brown water down the muddy slopes
Twisting its snake-like threads through moss and leaves.
No singing birds now haunt this place,
Nor drifts of starred anemone,
But all the mottled eyes bulge out
From toadstools in the undergrowth.
Yet where rain falls slow through sparkless air
Trees died a thousand times in smoke and flame
And charcoal burners fed their pits of fire
With branches green as lizard skin;
Each morning saw the clearing blue with sacrifice,
Each night was red with dragons' tongues.
And once I held a chip of virgin charcoal in my hand
And wrote my shaky name upon a stone;
I felt the newness of its powdered touch,
Its blinded buds, its destined power.
And in their wattled huts the burners crouched
Sweating and grimed, like Aztec chiefs at war;
From dusk to dawn they conned the veering wind,
Drawing at upturned pipes or munching bread
As hazel, ash and alder dropped to dust.
But all is gone and every fire is dead;
This single round of turf the only epitaph.
Yet one remains to look upon the wasted scene;
His shoulders hunched with sacks, an old man stands
With silver hair half hid in leaves and mist,
And sees himself a dancing boy again

Watching the ancient miracle that turned to black
By forest alchemy the tenderest green,
And hears above the well's small chattering tongues
The voices of old fiery boughs.

from ENGLISH MORNING AND OTHER POEMS (1953)

FAR HEADINGLEY

THE trees are dying in the gardens of the town,
Their heads, leafless and torn, look no more down
On lilied borders, fountains, and smooth, curving lawns
Nor hear the peacocks trumpet in the smokeless dawns.
The walls are tumbling of each urned and columned house
And sepulchred in dust lie withered bird and mouse.
Empty of life, remembering long forgotten sounds,
Shattered window-panes stare out on shattered grounds.
No longer do the walks and drives on Sundays bear
Crinoline and parasol in coach and pair,
And where on windswept nights burned high the log-piled fires
Now trails the wild convolvulus, and wander briars,
And cold-eyed spiders twitch and weave on mildewed wood
Where hung embroideries and ormolu once stood,
And they who talked of woollen wealth are buried deep
In figured vaults, and sleep, unwept, their city sleep.
The trees are dying and the bearded men are dead,
All debts paid in full, all family prayers are said.

from ENGLISH MORNING AND OTHER POEMS (1953)

HEDGEHOG

    for Andrew Young

LAST night, poor urchin in the fading light,
You lay unchained behind a thornless hedge,
Gorged with a slippery fill of slug and snail,
Thinking, perchance, of coming winter air,
And where to curl yourself in cosy dream
When frost first glazed your eyes and quivering snout;
The grasses broke their shadows on your back,
Dew fell on dusty beetle, hollowed leaf.
But when the moon came out to view the sky
With roving eye of longer sight than yours,
Then calm and dignified as any fabled beast,
You walked on moss and over crackling twig
On guard to hide yourself, to lift your spines,
To meet a sudden foe with armoured ball;
You walked into a noisy land of death,
And there, this morning, on the granite road,
Your little, flattened body slowly bled,
An arch of mocking freedom overhead.

from ENGLISH MORNING AND OTHER POEMS (1953)

THE THIEF
for Henry Treece

THE night before they nailed me to the sky,
In prison dream I saw the Devil as a bear
Walking up and down the world with fiery breath
And laying about him with knout and morning star,
And then myself, slow-festering in a scorpioned ditch,
Where Death had spewed me from his mouth,
With jellied back and hammer-shattered legs.
He spied me there and slyly changed his form
From red-toothed bear to meek-eyed, smiling lamb
And licked my wounds with cooling tongue.
And as from haunted sleep in fear I woke
He whispered like a dove into my ear,
 "And thou shalt hang on His left hand
   And He shall save thee."

from ENGLISH MORNING AND OTHER POEMS (1953)

VILLAGE IDIOT

THIS wind-blown scarecrow flutters with all rags flying
Over open fields, companion of first snow;
Behind him run dancing memories of last night's stars,
The picture of man-in-the-moon upside down in a rocking pool.
His head full of gold wisps and half forgotten tales,
He would, wind letting, make music to the sky
Or somersault his heart over haystack clouds.
Next year when children come to goggle at him over tadpole
    and net,
And then with trembling lip or giggle race away
Into a cuckoo land of hawthorn trees,
He'll range these fields again
Ennobled with dangling daisy crowns, wandering in weed,
Babbling his dictionary of backward words
To his sane self beneath the understanding sun.
He calls no plot of land his own, he cannot write his name,
Yet, lord of toads and master of small birds,
He has angels balancing on needles in his eyes,
And round his skull, heaven's madmen praising God
In secret psalms and songs.

from SELECTED POEMS 1940-1957 (1957)

THE PARK

THIS plot of grass, his world's end,
These shadowy pools, all his seas,
He stands, stocky and sure, no higher than a bush,
Inheriting the holy air,
Daisy, sun, the shy, uncurling leaf,
Taking to himself upon this ground,
Life's ease and friendly testament.
His heart beats wild at the waggling of a worm,
At the dropping of gold dust from the gillyflower,
He hears spring strike up the glad sound
When the snail slides from its wet stone,
And nods to the blackthorn cradling the happy thrush.
But now far down the enchanted slope
The city fades to sleep,
Paul's dome flashes to the stars;
He sighs, turns to his home again,
Bringing first sheaves with him.

from SELECTED POEMS 1940-1957 (1957)

LARKS AND CURLEWS

BEHIND a hedge upon a northern moor,
I watched through dripping thorn and leaf,
Some fields that pressed their heads
Against the tattered blackness of the sky.
Meadow-flowers hung waterlogged, grasses bent
Broken backs, scything half-drowned bees;
And from a bank of drunken fern
A draggled lamb stared woodenly at me.
And then from some bright nowhere in the clouds
A lark dropped down and stopped her song;
Another, still alive with Heaven, came
To sing awhile upon that rain-bedizened slope,
Until both skimmed away into a sea of undergrowth.
But as they disappeared from speckled view,
Two curlews streaked across the glassy land
Crying aloud with eager, double voice;
The larks were silent but the curlews called,
And sound and light had never died
Upon the movement of that battered air.

from SELECTED POEMS 1940-1957 (1957)

WILD PARSLEY

WHERE honeysuckle twines with bryony in the hedges
On Sark's roads twisting to the sea,
Wren and cricket weave sounds together,
And parsley, fool's flower of summer's madness,
Pushes white parasols over fern and pimpernel.
All night long while anemones sway with the tide,
These zany crowns rock, too, in solemn sleep,
Until the dying mackerel in the sky
Wakes the morning to dewy grass wands.
And when summer's fever is over
Parsley stems become marrowless autumn bones
And their blackening heads, poor simpletons,
Topple vacantly over into winter.

from SELECTED POEMS 1940-1957 (1957)

BONES

of fish, bird,
reptile, animal,
unseen, unheard,
one day shall
all be left behind,
litter on many shores,
or maybe find
graves on turfy moors,
skull of sheep,
last of the flock,
blanching on mountain steep,
rabbits' teeth turning to rock
with mammoth's thigh,
caveman's hunting horn
buried nearby,
and brooch carved for wedding morn.
And I have mine,
the three-and-thirty bones which are
my spine,
and make me perpendicular.
And so, a man, I stand
head in the sun,
feet firm on land,
safe in my living skeleton.

from FIELDS AND TERRITORIES (1967)

THE ROCKS

I PRESS my hand
flat upon the ground,
and know that underneath it are
the great rocks of the earth,
blackened and browned
clay and sand,
as at their birth,
when earth was a cooling star.
They lie band on band,
huge ribs of solid stone
with fossil of plant and bone.
And when I stand
alone upon this steadfast ground
I wonder why it was all planned,
and how the rocks came to be
after the earth was drowned,
and whether the sea was once all land,
the land, all sea.

from FIELDS AND TERRITORIES (1967)

BUTTON BOX

AN evening of wind and rain,
I found it on a shelf,
The button box, so full
Its lid would barely stay closed,
And opened it. Buttons.
Took them out one by one, all different
Shapes, sizes, colours, dull, thin;
Bone sometimes, and metal,
Holes, and none, some chipped,
A few leather, one had head of fox,
Another would do for dwarf's shield;
A dozen mother-of-pearl sang of the sea.
A set of silver ones
Might have been sixpences dancing,
A jet black handful
Went to grandfather's funeral, two
Only from mother's wedding dress,
Tiny, pink as rosebuds.
I turned them over and over, those buttons,
Our family there, laid out in rows,
Dotting the table, reflections in lamplight,
Then put them back, boy, girl,
Man, woman, warm from my fingers,
Into their cramped box,
Counted raindrops.

from FIELDS AND TERRITORIES (1967)

JANUARY

MONTH of owls, sagging all day
On dark rafters in mildewed barns,
Cutting though mist at nightfall, gulls
Greeting the morning plough, a thrush here and there,
Old nests balanced on bony branches, rooks
At noisy engineering on new ones, month when tender shoots
Begin to green sodden fields, catkins fire off
Gold powder, snowdrops christen the woods;
Month when brooks swell to brown rivers,
Coltsfoot surprises, groundsel is no weed.

from FIELDS AND TERRITORIES (1967)

SAMUEL PALMER AT SHOREHAM

CUTTING corn by night,
Moon lanterning, stars
Steady guides, we remembered last year's
Winnowings, smoking stubble, horses
Straining with jogging heads, and listening,
Harness bells jingling, a mouse
In turf rolling over in sleep.
Moving forward, west to east,
(The harvest following in its pleasure)
Hills opened out with pale gold;
Trailing in dew, suddenly stumbled on
Sacramental bread, saw
With unleavened eyes, stooks
In simple, great lines rise
Praising magnificently into Paradise,
Heard a lamb in brambles cry on the Son of God.

from WALKING WITH TREES (1970)

EXPRESSION OF COLOUR

I HAVE tried for a lifetime to express colour in words,
    communicate
Its exact sensation, tone, appearance;
In particular, of spring leaves, since first I became aware
There were leaves in my childhood forests.
But how to convey their veritable shade, degree of intensity,
This power has not been granted to me, it has
Passed me by, it will never be mine.
                                  Yet I know
Perfectly how light christens leaves, when
They are prisoners in shadow, how one leaf
Has at sunrise the same flush as
Its sleeping neighbour, in darkness,
The wash of moonlight.
                        But to be precise
To the point of astonishment, so that leaves
Are translated into green words, I have not that gift,
Who wanted it so, who needed it.

from WALKING WITH TREES (1970)

BOY AND GRASSES

THAT boy there, at the edge of the long grasses,
Trackless, figured with buttercup, unified by a solitary wind,
Grasps reality with fists full of cocksfoot and Yorkshire fog.
Then, with no backward glance to the safe house,
Sheds imprisoning clothes like a winding-sheet,
Parts the jungle with swimmer's hands, steps
Through winged air into thick growth;
A grasshopper leaps across his shadowed arm,
A snail, shaken from toppling perch,
Drops soundlessly into perilous dark;
The boy gives his weight to the bending green,
Wades on into the sea of full discovery,
Remembering no past, contemplating no future time;
For him the buried heart at Ujiji did not break in vain,
Nor shall the split atom speak only in curses for his generation.

He is gone, out of sight now;
Hidden by a humming forest of stems and seeds,
The world of his present engulfs him.
Stay, child, in safety there, until
The loved voice at the window points the way home
And you walk back, changeling of time, to be fettered again.

from WALKING WITH TREES (1970)

ASSEMBLY OF BIRDS

THESE birds, a wash of yellow, blue,
sit, silent-throated on silken stems,
caught for ever by time's fragility.
More alive this modern minute than
that porcelain morning when, alone,
absorbed, restrained, Huang-Chu'än painted them,
where bamboos stabbed the sun, pools
shimmered in amber, the landscape had no breath,
investing each stroke with essence of truth.
How calm they perch in more tranquil air,
feathers folded at rest, glowing in intensity.
I see them now through his slit eyes,
pick up a brush to seal their small mortality,
wait for a single note to fall,
echoing like silver rain-pearl
through fields and drowsing palaces,
the soft flutter of a wing, flash of vermilion,
myself at one with his, and their, repose,
the stillness of no time.

from SECRET AS TOADS (1972)

BULLFINCHES

THE season at its slow turn,
sun glinting through rain,
they suddenly come back
to their old plundering,
the bullfinch families,
kaleidoscopes of lustrous black,
breasts like danger lights,
a concentrated, fiery zodiac,
rasping at blossom-buds,
cherry, apple, and peach,
in gardens, or in quick hedges,
as if all nature were on the rack.
They flit in solitary companies
through leafy branches,
no word of command, attack
green tips of greener territories,
forage round thistle and haystack,
splitting the husked seeds,
fields littered with their bric-a-brac.
Delicate in love, are failed singers,
notes too breathlessly blown,
have never learned the knack
of composing a full song.
Linnaeus at Uppsala saw them,
those strange bullfinches,
flame into his almanac,
gazed long at such a paradox,
each beak, an iron thorn,
each cheek, a velvet rose.

from SECRET AS TOADS (1972)

BADGER

I WAIT in my fear at the edge of the wood,
the evening mild, the round moon
rising bland over the familiar hill.
All day I drowsed in the warm sett,
curled up in troubled dream
on matted grass and fern,
the silver cubs gone,
not daring to come out for the night walk.
And she, hanging dead and alone,
upside down on the spiked wire,
badge streaked with old blood,
torn flesh fermenting round smashed skull.
I heard her scream to the deaf stars,
brute cudgels beating the small life out,
her agony into my ears,
the red-eyed torches deceiving the dark,
dry leaves crackling beneath enemy feet.
I shiver here in my lonely fur, lift
my nose high for betraying scent,
find none, shuffle back home,
not wishing to play, roll by myself
along the moon's path, head-over-heels.
Her glassy eyes seem to search me out,
but must go on, groping for roots, snails,
keep company with wasp grubs,
spring-clean when the weather turns,
her bones picked white in murdered air.

from SECRET AS TOADS (1972)

MUSHROOMS

SECRET as toads. After a night's rain,
rise with the sun, dawn's flush on pillar and dome;
stronger than daisied turf, push into the light,
swell in an hour, tight, complete.
Summer's late harvest, miracles of white,
button up meadows, cool in the hill folds,
older than caveman wandering his wilderness.
Nothing more holy, live with manna's touch,
they shine, dew-crowned and comfortable.
And then, before final cockcrow fades,
ungathered and overblown in every hiding place,
wearily topple over on blackened stalks,
drenched with decay, worms in the soggy flesh.
By afternoon, dwindled to dust,
the mystery gone with the dew.

from SECRET AS TOADS (1972)

THE ELEMENTS

WHATEVER you feel about them you cannot change
The elements of the season.
Of course, in the interests of history you can rearrange
Them to suit your purpose, find a convincing reason
For doubting their significance, dismiss the whole thing
As a sentimental legend for the gullible young.
You can do all these, and angels on the wing
Will not stop you, though devils continue to prime your tongue.

The simple elements of the season remain, and are these;
A stable, a star, shepherds coming in from the wild,
Joining with kings on worshipping knees
To adore a new-born child.
But a very special child though,
Delivered then, as now, into a world of greed and hate.
(For all the holly and the mistletoe),
Doomed to rejection, then to a murderer's fate;
There's evidence enough to prove *that* act
And the birth and the death still going on and on.
Reverberating through Time, a ceaseless cataract
Of praise and prayer. And the star, too, has shone;
As if what took place on that particular night
Had never stopped, still quivered and hummed in the air,
Still burned and glowed in the light.
So do I gather myself together at this hour, wonderfully aware
That the elements of the season are prepared again for me,
And for all, in their mystical company.

from SINGING IN THE STREETS (1972)

EVERY VOICE

BREAK of day, in waving dream
I heard some fields whispering together,
grass blades bending beneath familiar skies;
it seemed every turf was trembling
with wordless praises.
Hunched hedges joined in the concord,
thorn thicket and bud murmuring,
trees, black and naked, scattered on hillsides
moved humming branches in a bleak wind,
the hills themselves, transported and shaking;
little earthquakes of adoration.
And soon, listening birds, fluffed in warm holes,
woke, with their chorus, hedgehog and shrew,
to snuffle carols of the damp mould:
every animal drowsy in stable and byre,
bellowing joy to jubilant stars;
the dead stirred in their graves,
birth and resurrection ruffling winding sheets,
the sun rising to a great crescendo.

Every voice was there,
my head full of the singing.

I cannot tell what mystery was sounding there,
at break of day, that rapturous morning:
I woke to its fading,
but knew, dead of winter, Love had been born again,
earth clamouring for unison with heaven.

from SINGING IN THE STREETS (1972)

PEACHES

THE house, Regency,
the walled gardens hushed in the sun,
tidy and formal as a page of Bach;
a few old peach trees
espaliered on the warm brick,
a line of little crucifixions facing south,
with victoria plums, comice pears.
Each velvet globe plucked from the branch,
precious as jewels, held to the cheek,
downy, softer than fawn's coat,
young girl's bloom, gently placed
in chip basket, still holding the day's heat.
And then the teeth sinking into firm flesh
deep to the furrowed stone,
honey juice dribbling down.
Think then of California, Virginia,
prodigal orchards ripening there,
peaches common as crab apples
littering the countryside all the days of fall,
feeding gross pigs, sweetening their hams,
trucks spilling over, or casually tossed
to rot in wasp-haunted heaps,
the air thick with smell of decay.
But here are rare and serenely beautiful,
the household glad and grateful at the sight
of twenty peaches on a September morning,
a child proud to be chosen for the first bite,
the garden sighing in the sun.

from THE BROAD ATLANTIC (1974)

LOOKING AT CORNFIELDS

FOR most of the day they dazzled, transfigured me,
My eyes were not used to the blaze of their light,
They seemed to belong to some holy mythology
With the whole of the landscape turning to white;
I thought I was looking at my immortality
And dreamed of it deeply for most of the night.

I lived with the living from morning till evening,
In those simple fields I took of the bread;
As the sun slowly made to his final westering,
The mystery of corn was interpreted,
And I come at last to my peaceful harvesting,
And roused by first cockcrow I rose from the dead.

from THE BROAD ATLANTIC (1974)

BEES

i

BEES do not follow fashion,
subscribe to earth's laws,
are ignorant of man's whims.

This morning's bees behaved golden,
like those that honeyed Samson's lion,
made Olympus wildly hum, swarmed
in Shakespeare's garden, saw Cortez
marching grimly through Mexican forests.

This evening's bees murmured when Rome fell,
whispered a victory song in Charlemagne's ear,
moved forward in clouds with Genghis Khan,
ravaging the steppes, lulled smocked villagers
dozing in hay fields at seeded summer.

Bees live the minutes for themselves,
servants of their own wax empires,
trespassers and secret travellers.

ii

You can hear them softly at first light,
foraging unseen in clover fields.
You can see them plundering the late limes,
when all else is dream, slow shadows.
You can smell bees each smokey harvest,
loaded and dipping towards packed hives.
You can touch them, curled up and motionless,
suddenly chilled by the frost.

from THE BROAD ATLANTIC (1974)

BEAR

DO NOT interfere with me;
I like to mind my own business.
If you hunt me down,
I shall outwit you, guns and all,
confuse you with false trails,
wait, affronted, in ambush,
until you pass by, then
charge with my 1500 fat pounds,
muscle and gold-brown fur,
red jaws ready to tear.
I am strong as rocks in Alaska.

Can send you flying with a blow,
senseless, from hammer claw,
pick up a whole deer,
carry secretly away, quiet as mouse,
through forest undergrowth,
shuffling my six-foot length along,
muzzle to printed ground,
swinging from side to side,
plenty of time in the world.

Keep away your dogs, too,
Can crush them to pulp
Between forepaws and ribs.
I am nasty when roused.

But do not see well,
eyes weak, too small,
can smell you out, though,
coarse scent on the wind,
or honey lodged in tree.

Am a fine climber,
balance better than acrobat,
on branches that take my weight;
sure head for heights,
not scared of mountain ledge;
a powerful swimmer,
lakes are all mine in summer,
loll silly in the sun.

I enjoy my own company,
am no great traveller,
but know the best places for roots,
sweet berries, grubs in old logs.
I live for green corn fields,
grapes at wine harvest,
very greedy for young salmon
silvering the July creeks,
will stuff myself with them,
chewing only the best bits.
I like a good joke.

And when the weather turns,
hills whiten with first flakes,
find some cave, hole in the ground,
block up entrance with trees,
any old rubbish, curl up,
caught in the season's sleep,
whatever winds may howl,
snow drift in the crevices,
drowse the long winter away,
getting leaner and leaner.

The cubs are born then;
she keeps them from me.

I do not mind, am too tired
to bother with them,
toothless and blind,
naked in the warm den.
She licks them one by one,
later will cuff them hard,
make them obey.

When icicles break,
I move off across the slopes
my father padded on,
thin as starved stoat,
thinking of redskin braves.
They worshipped all bears once,
begged their pardon, wept
when it came to the knife
and skin for the back.

I yawn away time,
A new sun shines,
rivers and woodlands call,
beetles and marmots creep out,
bees are at work for me.

from THE BROAD ATLANTIC (1974)

CAVE PAINTING

OUT in the wild marsh an old bull stands
white and forlorn, bellowing to the stars;
heifers splash on through mud and salted weed,
ignoring his demand. A dozen colts, mouths free,
gallop with the wind along the hill's edge;
a branched stag moves from dark trees,
laps water from a pool, delicately sniffs the air,
retreats soundlessly to tangled forest, boars
snort, fiery-eyed in damp undergrowth, mammoth's shadow
falls across trampled ferns and grasses.

Down in the safe cave with beaker and arrow-head
the low-skulled tribe huddle together in moist dream.
Tomorrow, when sun-god wakes to warming speech,
tunnel's end becomes a hemisphere of light,
children finger meatless marrow bones,
women keen at their grinding, hunters creep out,
muttering magic words, with stone axe and spear,
steered by hunger into a fearful world of beasts
lurking in dens, silhouetted on menacing cliff.

One stays, and by moss-wick's oily flame,
paints with carbons and ochres a long-maned horse,
tusked pigs, a swift running of red deer,
bison at bay, upon the limestone walls,
hand clenching stick, delighting in strength of limb,
harmony of movement, glowing life of skin.
But deeper still than heart's impulse,
the will to capture and to slay, flint buried in back,
head severed, dragged back to evening's fire,
the conquered one, possessed and sacrificed.

And this small child, silent and primitive,
who now draws mysteries with crayon or familiar brush,
such mild-eyed sheep in meadow, horse and cow,
how can he know how close he is to that furred man
worshipping at rock face, loving the colours and forms,
those bloodstained hunters rejoicing at the kill?
And does he feel some quickening of the blood,
and innocent fingers reaching for a knife?

from THE BROAD ATLANTIC (1974)

GRASS

'WHAT is grass?' the child asked,
and Whitman gave a poet's answer,
explaining nothing. Dürer
painted a clump of it,
formal and brilliant in German air.
I ask the same question now,
looking out on winter pastureland,
but can only find a rational answer,
am more ignorant than the child.
Blake could have interpreted it for me,
Samuel Palmer, ecstatic and dazzled at Shoreham.

And yet I know grass almost by heart,
its touch, colour and rare scent,
common, yet strangely individual,
beautiful and everlasting from the beginning of time,
since first I rolled down childhood hills,
my body scented with summer,
the strong life entering me.

And how many times have I heard them chime,
the belled quaking grasses, in a soft wind,
a delicate peal for unencumbered days;
or walked, a green and wondering man,
through small forests of cocksfoot, foxtail,
red darnel, brown bents and brome,
sniffed sweet vernal in old hayfields,
the mowers moving westward with the sun;
held a broad blade of couch grass
between stuff thumbs, blown a sharp note
over river banks, scattering dragonflies;

threaded stems with wild strawberries,
spattering their blood all the way home.

Barley and oat shall cover me at the end,
my dust become panicks and fescues.

Rain falls, the grasses silently grow,
larks hide their pearled songs in the dark growth,
alien with sorrel and chamomile,
pimpernel holds up its poor man's weather glass;
a lost village is buried deep, flint and coin,
a king's bones blanch beneath matted roots,
cattle and cannon tracks photographed on turf.

Grass is my security,
my firm hold on time,
that takes me, hour by hour,
from flying husk and seed
to dry flakes at my dark end.
I never see a solitary tuft
lodged with the frost in pavement cracks,
but feel its hidden power
to burst from the prison holes,
grotesquely swell and break the stone,
cover the ruined world again
with huge, primeval fields,
savannah, prairie and steppe,
running from mountains to the sea,
shining and undefiled.

I sense the potency of that tuft in me.

from THE BROAD ATLANTIC (1974)

SMALL LIFE

FISH in ice do not feel snowflakes
drifting on glassed stream, hears
thin shrew suddenly scuffling
a few hungry minutes through reeds,
sharp-nosed fox on iron bank
sniffing scentless air, corn mouse,
drowsy-eyed in bare field
retreating to hedge hole, foraging hedgehog,
frost in spines, lumbering out of ditch.
Mole, clay-bound in chill velvet,
blind to fish in ice, shrew, ravenous fox,
deaf to twitching mouse, hedgehog.
Small life, lonely and ignorant, breathes winter away,
waits slowly for sun's fingers, greening copse
spilling over with fresh singers, soft rain showers;
has visions only of seed, slug, dancing fly,
leveret uncertain, in upland form.

from THE BROAD ATLANTIC (1974)

HILLS

HAVE names, shadows,
farms tilted in the green folds,
rain driving the sheep along thin tracks
into mists that lose themselves near the sky.
Hills have curlews crying, heather
rolling purple tides with singing bees
over and over, up, down;
and thyme drugging summer's small air.
Snow lingers in crevices, hides all wounds
an extra month or more, winter streams
tumble with loud voices into the valleys,
there are trees carved by the wind.

Hills should not be ploughed, let grass
rule them with rock and solitude,
the dead sleep on in their long barrows,
let hills be, rabbit and hawk
fight out time together.

from THE BROAD ATLANTIC (1974)

MOLE

CURLED up in leafy fortress, secure,
I am the little black lord of the underworld.
proud and solitary in my tight plush;
prince of the sappers I have excavated the whole of Europe,
hills and tunnels advertising me all the way to Japan.
My four strong ounces drive forward at speed,
long, whiskered snout ramming the stones and roots,
leaving the damp night-tubes behind,
sun and wind unfriendly aliens
as I lift up the earth into the cruel light,
clawing out worms and grubs, gorging myself.

I do not see well but can sniff out stoats,
hear lightest footsteps hunting overhead,
will fight to the death with needle teeth,
once killed a sour king;
am not interested in my naked young.

Winter comes, I go down deeper
into my freezing element; do not sleep.
No fool, I am fearful of farmers, cunning traps,
the indignity of transfixion on bush and wire.

I am a strange character,
persistent and quarrelsome;
you would miss me though if I disappeared for ever
with dodo and dinosaur.

Better leave me alone to my dark moods.

from THE BROAD ATLANTIC (1974)

ENGLISH COUNTY

A LAND of old hills beneath wide skies,
a crazed pattern of fields, pasture and corn,
high hedges overhanging lanes of campion and hartstongue,
trees dotted over the speckled landscape, and farms
tucked in hollows, flotillas of clouds;
a land out of time, solemn with silent witnesses.

The sun eases away the last drops of dew,
cows move with their shadows out of steaming milking sheds,
a flock of gulls dips in from the sea,
settle as one bird along stubbled lines,
a tractor puffs away the morning,
crisp barley gathered in;
a man strides with dog and gun across the slopes.

A vision of innocence, fresh as rainwater,
childhood returned again with warm, dead voices;
Samuel Palmer saw it at Shoreham in stooklight,
Wordsworth among his lakes, Thoreau in hickory woods,
Clare's poems dropped with his sweat on holy turf;
Beethoven heard it in bird song, his ears unstopped,
Michaelangelo, upsidedown in the Sistine Chapel.

I breathe some of its divinity now,
am washed by it as these hills are washed,
know that Love is shining here, everlasting;
give back what quickens my heart,
kindles my dulled eyes;
and have a taste of harvest honey on my tongue.

from THE BROAD ATLANTIC (1974)

THE PEA-PICKERS

TRAVELLING north, a glazed afternoon in June,
the train slowed down, and stopped. Lincolnshire,
and men and women picking peas in flat, hot fields.
I watched them in their bended silence, a few minutes or so,
moving forward in ragged lines from row to row,
beneath a huge, unbroken sky. Pea-pickers.

They wore the same grave face as their ancestors,
prisoners of the land, who worked these meadows
all weathers, fingers in frost, rain whipping bowed backs,
from turnip-hoeing to barley-time,
bonnetted grandmothers, babies humped in hedges,
long-pinafored, with wooden dolls from Peterborough Fair.

The signal dropped. We started up again.
They did not notice it, continued following the sun,
locked in the solitude of timelessness.
I thought of Clare, soaked through with dew,
picking with them, first light to sundown,
poems in his wild eyes, lonely for love;
and Cobbett, caustic and critical, riding these fields,
stuffing his head with figures and facts.

But most of the great cycle of the years,
morning at seed-time, starlight at harvest,
peas planted, butterfly flowers, tangles of tendrils,
pods swelling, haulm withering to death.

And if, by chance, this time next year,
I should come this way,
these old acres would be new again with peas,

pickers still dumb and stooping there,
patiently moving forward, baskets crammed,
the self-same rhythm, season after season,
life, death, and resurrection.

from THE BROAD ATLANTIC (1974)

EYES AND VOICES

EYES watching.
                I see them now
searching me out in this half-light murmur
where evening's stars put small windows in dark trees;
a surveillance of glances, lonely and questioning,
moves along soft-breathing borders,
calling me to sleep
and young lovers in avenues under
parallels of cool limes, humming with heavy bees.
The eyes are unwavering.
                        I do not flinch from their gaze.
Let them be blind to the ugly visions of present time.
They peer from dead skulls,
witnesses of yesterday
I remember in the sunlight,
pince-nez with lorgnette, fichus and spidered veils.
They are all watching.

And voices.
            I hear them now
speaking to me in this half-heard silence
where morning's sun prints first shadows on diamond lawns;
a sprinkle of words, lively and loving,
falls through drowsed summer air,
calling me from sleep
and hidden birds in woods beyond
lines of old fields, green-bladed with new corn.
The voices are insistent.
                            I cannot escape from their echoes.
Let them be silent to the harsh babel of present time.
They sound from dead lips,
whisperers of yesterday

I remember in the shadows,
panama with cartwheel, blazers and silk blouses.
They are all speaking.

And voices have eyes,
eyes, voices.

from THE HEARING HEART (1974)

CHILDREN OF ISLINGTON

THEY creep out of shabby houses in long back-streets,
Inhabit a kingdom of desolate places,
The day's wild fury continually throbs and beats,
Night's fever written deep on pinched-up faces.

They seem to have passed beyond the world's loving care,
As if childhood itself suddenly had stopped,
Their innocence doomed, wilting away in the public glare,
And over each a cage of misery has dropped.

They know too much of sadness, vulnerable and young,
Will not all come to a season of full flower,
Nor shall a spontaneous song lie rejoicing on every tongue,
To flood the firmament with a vision of power.

There is small comfort here for these castaways, where
Sour rooms breed resignation behind cracked panes,
A babel of quarrelling voices bludgeons the frenzied air,
And grief goes dumb and sullen whenever the sky rains.

And yet upon their drooping heads a little sunlight falls,
Whose beams are stronger far than laws and politics,
And when across the roofs a bird at morning calls,
There is a glory on the black and crumbling bricks.

They dawdle back at evening to the clamour of the slums,
That greed and gracelessness have long contrived;
What hand can turn these festering wastes to new Elysiums,
And not a single child neglected and deprived?

from THE HEARING HEART (1974)

DE LA MARE'S BELL

THIS was de la Mare's bell,
Brass, reflecting what it imaged,
Minute, distorted, upside down,
The handle, a black minaret on its tower,
Its tiny tongue,
Time's clapper, tinkling like glass inside.

It used to rest on the table by his bed,
With flowers, a clock, and books
Unopened or half read.
I often saw him lift it gently up,
The old fingers twining round the wood,
Then shake it into dulcimer sound,
Very kind and pleasant to the ear,
Its voice chiming clearly through the Twickenham house;
A few charmed seconds, and then
The bell was brought to dumbness, the air was still,
The Roman head sank back to rest;
It was all over.

And I used to think how like de la Mare his bell was,
Fragile, haunting, sure, precise,
Sounding boards for dream and the indefinable.
And now, de la Mare dead, the flowers dead,
The clock counting out life elsewhere,
My son rings the bell,
Rings it, not for a poet's passing or curfew for night,
Rings it, innocent bellman, through childhood's frail house,
Through twilight, moonlight, the soft shades,
Listening forests of stars,
The dusty pavilions of Time.

But, O, if I rang till doomsday's crack
I could not bring him back.
Let this blithe bellman ring.

from THE HEARING HEART (1974)

IN NORFOLK

AT the back of the principal marsh,
stockades of reed and rush, river-green,
smooth cornfields flow in tawny tides
up and down the landscape, out of sight.
Wafered butterflies float the untroubled air,
a pheasant treads out of the straw shade,
jewelled and arrogant into the sun's firm eye;
it is a sacramental afternoon.
And I have come to my safe lodging here
in the hallowed light of harvest,
as if all Knapton's angels were flying over me,
these fields flaming with cherubim;
I am one with Breughel's immortal reapers,
praying their sickled way to evening,
I stand redeemed in golden meadows,
Blake's New Jerusalem.

I pluck a single ear of corn,
feel its strong divinity,
a barley-needle draws my blood,
and I am lifted up.

from THE HEARING HEART (1974)

HEDGEHOG

COMES out by day in autumn,
exploring hedgehog, betrays himself
snoring loudly in leafy ditch;
plump with summer's fat, moves along,
battering slow way through dry twigs.
I hear him lumbering, hairy head appears,
then all his ten-inch prickly length,
makes for the bank, senses me there,
rolls into a ball, waits for the attack.
I leave him alone though, curled up on the hill's lip,
this earth-brown savage, enemy of frogs.
He'll chew beetles and mice to powder, hear
every small noise in undergrowth,
will take on snakes by the tail,
bayonet them with needle-spines.
Shy of the sun, dislikes company,
cannot see far, a fine swimmer,
drinks milk.

from THE HEARING HEART (1974)

FALLOW

THE light is Dutch light, clear, serene;
the old masters knew it, Ruisdael and Avercamp,
Vermeer at Delft, January afternoons,
spring at sleep in their palette-boxes,
frost hung fresh on muted grass,
vermilion sun folding up over black dykes,
as now it picks out this one field,
flooding it for an hour or so with ochre.
A few hungry birds peck at nothing,
skeleton hedges have short shadows,
a broken harrow rusts away time.

The field is fallow,
lines clean, and waiting,
life working silently beneath the turf;
on either side, plumed kale, viridian,
new furrows, dark as umber.

And lovers, too, have their seasons of fallowness,
when fires are low, yet still are glowing there,
a time to rest, mellow and silent;
waiting secure, in winter's sunlight,
another seeding, a fuller harvest.

The old masters knew it.

from THE HEARING HEART (1974)

IX

WORKING on an old poem late at night,
nothing would come, could not say
what I wanted to say, page after page
scrawled over with sterile graffiti.
I put the thing away, defeated, labour in vain,
angered I had not sized up to the skill,
the foetus still in my head, no separate life.
Came back after sleep with more calm,
craved for release, stared at a blank wall.
Mind wandering, then thought of you
waking with love at sunrise now
somewhere out of my range;
was charged again.

The poem changed shape, flowed at my will,
The seed grew, came to flower, I saw the fruit,
The word made flesh.

A lover in my arms, I was at one with the words,
was with you.
How strange a conception that you at that hour
had delivered my child.

from SILENCE OF THE MORNING (1978)

XIX

IRON man, speak to me
from your litter of bone and shard,
where now on summer turf I lie alone,
brooding, perplexed,
beneath your graveyard hill,
breathing this valley's unbearable silence.
Speak to me of the frosted days,
the starved tribe huddled together for warmth,
fearful under dumb stars,
horses whinneying in the long dark,
snow levelling the maze of ditches and banks.
Speak,
you who lolled away
the summer minutes in thyme-scented grass,
scabious trembling, cattle
shadowing the carved slopes,
skylarks singing over water and wood below.
How was it with you then?
What unseen terrors clutched at your throat
each fevered night among embers and sling stones,
waiting for the god at morning to shine?
Speak, furred man,
I have no comfort here,
millenials of grief away from you,
no answers to any questions I ask myself
before my tears turn to iron.

Living man, I do not understand,
and did not ever know.
I felt only the wind's blade,
the wild assault of the rain on my skull,
and saw the brooch I made for her,

fading in cold hand,
my eyes remembering.
I met each labyrinthine day as it came,
went to my lonely end.
I took what I could while it was,
gave back what was given me,
held in my tears.
Living man, live,
love on.

from SILENCE OF THE MORNING (1978)

RETREAT TO SILENCE

RETREAT to silence
here, now, at this moment,
where only the stones speak,
the moted air
sings in strange syllables,
that you may in some part
hear with your whole being
what they have to say to you.

Listen to them,
you, who come to this place
unaware of what it has to give;
they have not retreated to silence
but will give you the words
you cannot find yourself
for your prayers.

from 12 POEMS FROM ST BARTHOLOMEW'S (1978)

GREEN MAN WANDERING

A GREEN man wandering all his days
with foxes running red in twilight
through frosted fern, deer standing motionless
in the moon's liquid eyes by antlered trees,
pin-point of a morning kestrel circling between hills;
wanders all seasons, all weathers.

Head bared to the wind's hammer he walks
in wondering silence the flowering land
of blackthorn breaking out of winter,
knots of primroses hunched under deep hedges,
floats with first royal butterfly,
swims the great drowning flood of bluebells.

Not crazed, but jubilant,
his ears are tuned to the cuckoo's clock,
eyes for flash of kingfisher, trout
imprisoned for a rainbow moment
between wimpling water and air.

He takes the frogged pools with him,
dragonflies and marsh marigolds,
into the daisied meadows of summer,
ploughs slowly on to harvest,
the whole earth ripening for him,
the heavens.

And when the larks rise to the sun,
singing the warm songs of apple trees,
he puts on the new clothes of the resurrection,
in a twinkling becomes a grass blade,
is mossed all over with immortality,

dances with scarecrows and shooting stars,
shares his secrets only with laughing bees.

A green man,
wandering.

from THE WAY IT WAS (1980)

CIDER-HOUSE

THE farmer died fifty years ago,
no child to follow him, the family name
remembered only on a lichened line of gravestones,
one on the war memorial in the north aisle;
the weeds inherited, mildew in the long barn,
bats dangling from rotting beams, blackened ricks,
holes in the thatched shippen,
stars shining through.

New tenants came with silos, tractors,
doubled the cows in the valley meadows,
ten score of sheep balanced on the hills;
left the cider-house empty.
Mice scuttle now through cobweb and moonbeam
where once the little engine purred October mornings away,
the air half-drugged with sweet fumes,
the cutter rusted, the press shrunken and dry.

Only a few remember the cider days,
the shuffle of clogged feet on the littered floor,
fruit piled high in the round baskets,
trundled in from the warm harvesting,
the nodding horses waiting patiently by the orchard gate,
waggons bumping along the ruts to the cool house.

And then all day the golden liquid
trickling, bubble and drop, through the creaking wood,
the engine still humming the same, soft song,
pipes, hogsheads and puncheons filled to the bung,
the raw juice heady, overflowing,
mashed straw and pulp thrown to the pigs.

They are gone now, cider-house and orchards,
the billowing tides of blossoms riding the slopes,
with early bees raiding, and Severn, a silver eel,
twisting to the sea on the far-away skyline.

The magical names remain,
those old apples of cidered Gloucestershire,
Skyrmes Kernel, Dymock Red, and Forest Styre,
Black Foxwhelps and Redstreak;
such honeyed sounds,
pure English poetry in my country ears.
I say each one to myself now, lovely on my tongue,
as ripe and rounded as cider itself,
drunk with long memories from a china mug,
the fire glowing on a winter evening.

from THE WAY IT WAS (1980)

BIOLOGICAL EXPERIMENT

A DEAD frog cannot be quickened into being,
renew the trembling and battle of creation
along the quadrant of his limbs;
the current to do this would have to come
from a dynamo, not from a small volt battery.

Yet, somewhere, there must be a needle,
pregnant and sharp enough,
to push into the frog's faint beating muscles
and waken them, if only in holiday mood,
into some bitter kind of idiocy.

The marsh with its foulness waits, the rushes
claim the last communion of its broken body;
one would need the accumulated energy of a million power stations
working against time, to bring back the shape,
the old pattern of its breathing.

Too late now, or too soon;
this bottled frog has become an insignificant part
of the waste of frustration,
which, in itself, is indestructible.

from THE WAY IT WAS (1980)

STILL BORN

I CARRIED you in hope,
the long nine months of my term,
remembered that close hour when we made you,
often felt you kick and move
as slowly you grew within me,
wondered what you would look like
when your wet head emerged,
girl or boy, and at what glad moment
I should hear your birth cry,
and I welcoming you
with all you needed of warmth and food;
we had a home waiting for you.

After my strong labourings,
sweat cold on my limbs,
my small cries merging with the summer air,
you came. You did not cry.
You did not breathe.
We had not expected this;
it seems your birth had no meaning,
or had you rejected us?

They say that you did not live,
register you as still born.
But you lived for me all that time
in the dark chamber of my womb;
and when I think of you now,
perfect in your little death,

I know that for me you are born still;
I shall carry you with me for ever,
my child, you were always mine,
you are mine now.

Death and life are the same mysteries.

from THE WAY IT WAS (1980)

MAURICE

HE reads the weather in the country signs,
printed, dawn and dusk, on wooded hills,
the changing face of stream and sky;
hears all the village news on his private wind,
takes it around with him, fair or foul,
sharing it with friends who gladly come
to greet him in his favourite, welcoming inn,
enjoying the pleasure of his jovial company.

A gentle man, no cynicism in him,
his help is freely given, early or late,
his head so full of enterprises and schemes
that, carol singing over, summer's fête begins;
haymaking to harvest the meadows know him.

As innocent as the daisies, new and white,
which star the churchyard turf in spring,
and, where, one day the news will be
that he has joined the lines of those who knew his worth;
the sun shall bless him, the remembering rain
not wash away the simple record of his deeds.

He will lie there in peace, at home,
bell sounds floating high over him,
bees murmuring on the wing,
grasses waving his name,
the young trout rising.

from THE WAY IT WAS (1980)

RECTOR

WOULD have been at home in any century,
this good-humoured priest, adapted well to each;
natural qualities include patience,
ability to spot the counterfeit,
courage to condemn it.

Think of him in the late eighteenth,
going the parish rounds, country or city church,
scholar's hood worn lightly, bands and wig,
preaching the word, comforting the sick,
sitting late at night in candle-lit study,
honouring the Book of Common Prayer;
of the faithful company of Donne and Herbert,
but affinities, too, with the English mystics;
would have been acceptable, without a doubt,
at Parson Woodforde's dinner table;
has a fund of anecdotes.

Enough of the visionary in him to see angels
walking through Smithfield at their ease,
enough of the evangelical to raise no alarm
at York or Canterbury, a Broad Churchman,
lodged happily here for forty years
with Norman pillars, arches and aisles;
a perfect musical setting.

For all his knowledge of theology,
there is a heart beating warm beneath that red cassock,
and a rebel struggling to break out in fury

against the machinations of systems and hierarchies;
and has done so on occasions.

Rahere, of course, knows most about him,
and will speak in due time.

from THE WAY IT WAS (1980)

SERMONS IN STONES

LONG dead to village gossip and lies,
the Reverend Samuel Wallis, Master of Arts,
Vicar of Loders and Bradpole, 1820-1835,
buried here, a grey stone slab on the choir,
'With Molly, his wife';
no other details.

There was whispering and scandal enough,
all the commandments broken, a self-righteous age,
when Samuel ranged these parish fields,
visiting the sick, the tardy church-goer,
the same lies told, the same calumny;
men and women do not change
whatever monarch or weather rules.

And did he close his ears,
bury himself alive in classical studies,
the vicarage fires comfortably burning?
Pray for lost souls on threadbare knees?
Or thunder forth iniquities,
lumping sinners and saved together?
And all without profit.

We shall never know,
there are no records of him,
the kind of man he was,
lion or lamb;
it has no consequence.

A particle of dust now,
Samuel Willis is floating freely in Dorset air,
his ministry forgotten.

The chattering tongues live on.

from THE WAY IT WAS (1980)

THE WAY IT WAS

THEY all knew, but said nothing,
those watching ones, company of friends,
standing still and impassive there;
an open secret, they showed no signs
that Love was breathing in that place
where bells sang, soft light fell.
The two did not look at each other
but, darting shy glances at the calm faces,
wondered if in their courtesy they guessed
the way it was with them;
for all their agreed discretion,
their innocence gave the game away;
lovers' eyes do not lie.
The others were happy for them,
sharing the unsaid rapture of their joy.
Even when the two slipped away,
the ringing over, into the muffled dark,
the others remained faithful,
kept their pact of delicate silence,
smiled wisely, talked of other things.
Such was the nature of their pure acceptance,
clear recognition without comment,
a true relationship understood,
needing no analysis.

And they together, alone with their mystery,
inheriting a common kingdom,
held hands like children,
the night enfolding them,
so transfigured they said nothing.

from THE WAY IT WAS (1980)

I

A LANDSCAPE of trees, massed
on little hills, a Roman phalanx
marching with the wind into hollows;
the woodlands, stockades,
encircling slated villages;
old coal mines, seams as waterlogged
as the lungs of those who sweated them,
coughing their breathless way into packed churchyards;
and two rivers, west, east,
silently twisting through plum and sheep country
on muddy way to the sounding channel.

There I grew up in my sapling years,
wandering freely all seasons, day and night,
a solitary, stumbling through foxgloved fern,
or over frosted fields at owl-light;
content with my condition
did not think of any future.

But now, gripped by the fever of homesickness,
return for a timeless hour or so;
the landmarks changed, lose my way,
realise I no longer belong here,
recognise only a few lined faces,
though family names still shout at me.

And wonder, this summer-humming afternoon,
what impelled me to go home.
Was it to walk abroad with the dead?
Discover again roots that may never have been there?
Or the foolishness of age in late rebellion?

There are no answers.
But brought back with me, almost unaware,
a landscape of tress, massed
on little hills.

from AN INTIMATE LANDSCAPE (1981)

III

ALMOST no history,
the town, bleak, bare,
little more than a jigsaw of small houses,
shops, grey chapels and churches, sprawled,
a monstrous fossil,
across a westward-looking hillside,
marshland clogging the valleys;
summer-scorched, winter biting hard,
it was hacked out of moor and old forest.
You could explore it in an hour.

Little beauty of itself,
though cottage gardens blazed,
midsummer sunsets flooded the long slopes,
and a new architecture flowered when snow came;
only its setting gave distinction
with house rising upon house to dramatic skies;
poverty walked the roads with me,
the naked years of depression salting the air.
The fortunate escaped.

But always the comforting sight of trees,
oaks and beeches whichever way you turned,
half-hiding tall chimney shafts and tips;
and beyond them, far mountain ridges
keeping their alien secrets to themselves.

At the top of the town
where the wind always blew fresh and free,
a great panorama, the bowed river
sparkling through red meadows and farms,

the white cathedral tower commanding,
belonging it seemed to another country.

The river still curves to the sea,
the woodlands throb with song,
but the town has changed,
more prosperous, cosmetic,
almost like any other town.
I remember its drabness but also its pride;
the faces of the colliers have all been washed white
and something fierce and passionate gone.

My hope is I am given a last sight of it all,
skies, fields, riverbank and glade,
before I am finally tidied up for the night.

from AN INTIMATE LANDSCAPE (1981)

V

IT was the warm smell of honeysuckle
I best remember, spicing the quick hedgerows,
and dog roses, pink and white tangles;
stems intertwined they hid blackbirds' nests.

Their fragrance and dazzle are with me now
as, early morning, I explore another landscape
with rambling arches of honeysuckle and dog roses.
But this is not my country;
it does not speak a familiar language,
and she who once lingered with me,
halting at the far stile to take breath,
long dead to summer's songs,
is walking, too, another country.

from AN INTIMATE LANDSCAPE (1981)

IX

IT was an orchard of plum trees
massed on a turfed hillside
where rabbits and sheep ran.
You came to it from a chestnut wood
along the carters' wheel-scored track
to another part of the forest.

Those trees heaved to the springtime skies,
heavy with blossom and bees,
a backcloth of white magnificence;
and, at picking time, such mellowness,
with propped-up branches loaded,
long ladders reaching up to the sun,
round, flannel-shirted men dressed for the occasion,
very gently placing the warm fruit into wide baskets
as if they were newly-laid eggs.

No orchard now
as I come this way again,
a day in winter,
frost gripping the track;
and the old plum-pickers
packed away in their churchyard boxes.

The hillside is a new world,
bricked cottages where the orchard once was,
television aerials, metalled road,
cars parked at every gate,
small formal gardens.

But no regrets.
No foolish grieving for what is gone;

it did not always glow in its own time.
There is only a change of scene,
and a different play being acted out.
But the roots of the trees still deep in me,
and, remembering white flowers,
I come to my picking time.

from AN INTIMATE LANDSCAPE (1981)

XII

WHEN the nights drew in, they quietly came back,
the gypsies, to their old camping ground,
a coppice, on the edge of the complacent town,
smoke from the slow fires circling around
patched covered wagons, tents black and brown,
into the larches, and across the railway track.
They kept to themselves in that one spot;
only the midwife or the policeman ever came
to see them squatting around each simmering pot,
or whittling wood for making toys and pegs,
with tattered children at some secret game,
or dancing like maenads through the leaves,
thin-faced, bare feet and legs;
they could not read and never went to school.
The town declared they were all rogues and thieves,
who did not work, or follow any rule,
but could tell fortunes by looking at your hand,
cure coughs and colds, cast spells.
I went to see them once, as to a foreign land,
not thinking they might spirit me away,
and there, with them, and their sweet, woody smells,
I stayed entranced for more than half the day.
They laughed out loud and gave me rabbit stew,
told many a daring Romany tale,
a young girl sang a song of travelling,
a crippled man spoke of his years in gaol,
and what to do with silver when the moon is new.

No gypsies came there now. The copse is felled.
The ones I met I never saw again,

and I have wandered far uncertainly,
but often feel that I have been expelled
from all the freedom of the sun and rain
once given to me by that blithe company.

from AN INTIMATE LANDSCAPE (1981)

XVIII

I MARVEL at it,
the annual resurrection of toads.

This morning's random spade-stroke
revealed one in the moist garden;
another, as rough and wrinkled,
trying to look invisible
beneath a shifted barrel.

By evening toads were everywhere,
crawling from under private stones and leaves
into the public eye,
falling clumsily into holes,
inviting sudden death on mad roads,
or merely squatting, strange and motionless,
breathing with closed mouths.

They look old,
as secret as the dark earth itself,
moving with passionate longing
to seek the water where they were born
as now, sluggish and slow,
I come at last to my maturity,
my low blood warming to your love,
stirring again to find my resurrection in you.

Hold me now, new and living, in your hands;
accept my warts and all.

from WINTER TO WINTER (1979)

XIX

THE land, a chessboard of brown squares,
Cold March, tight hands upon the sun,
Over the misty hills the lusty hares,
A dozen spring-heel jacks now madly run.
All else is still, and every meadow wears
An empty face, but take a closer look
And see the writing there in ordered lines,
The blades of seedling corn an open book.
Each gentle slope now swells and shines
With harvest promise, stook by stook,
The green film thickens to a pile
And what was bare to general view
Becomes ribbed velvet, mile on mile,
And springtime printed clear on you.

from WINTER TO WINTER (1979)

THE FORTRESS

NOT the dramatic first sight of ruined towers
seen through a summer haze from the valley road
curling its blanched way uphill to San Gimignano
through silver olives, vines and black cypresses.
Not history-book recollections of faded Tuscan wars,
Guelph and Ghibelline factions, the jealous families,
Dante speaking fire to the Council in the Town Hall,
swaying the citizens to action against their will.
Not the dead cistern in the baked piazza,
the twin-coloured columns of the cathedral,
Sebastian waiting patiently for the gift of another arrow,
and Ghirlandaio painting his 'Annunciation',
dawn to dusk in St Augustine's cloister.

What was significant were the swallows and crows
circling the pinnacles, as if the princes
had come back to their quarrellings,
a school of gnarled old men playing cards
solemnly outside a wine-shop,
the latest rock song screaming from a window,
and a half-starved tom cat
slinking round a corner with frightened eye,
the chopped-off head of a cockerel in guilty mouth.

But a kind of security still,
no longer needing walls and towers.

from BURNT SIENA (1980)

WHEN SNOW FALLS

NO surprise after the raw day's bite,
snow should come at evening;
first fall of the year, drifted down all night
blown by a small wind, until, by morning,
everywhere, everything was blanketed;
a kind of transfiguration
with its own silence and architecture.

Such silence that the slightest sound
from bird cheeping on loaded branches
cut through the wounded air, went on echoing
long after the bird had flown;
such architecture, with new dimensions
of mathematics and geography created
in a few unclocked hours.

And I wondered if you, too, had expected snow,
watched the flakes floating, as I watched them.
Or did the changed weather catch you unawares
as Love, sometimes imperceptibly appears
bringing a white kingdom
not printed with old scars?

When snow falls again,
my hope we share that magnetic moment,
hear it speak with the same voice,
needing no interpreter.

Other Poems

SILENCE AND WATER

RAIN dropping from willow trees,
I came to a place of silence and water,
Crumpled your letter in cold hand,
Dropped it, a mourner at my own funeral,
Into the long grave of the stream;
The bruised paper fell dead, carried away
Beneath a black arch, all hope drowned.

Turned back then, the words printed on my eyes,
'I have no comfort for you.'
As if it were comfort I needed,
Or pity, but love.
There was a name written, too. I knew it.
It was not mine. You had more than comfort for him.

I walk the soaking fields in silence and water,
The name following me, stopping my ears;
Marooned in mist, I have no peace from it,
Your words magnified by the glass of the stream,
Skies weeping with unquenchable tears.
You, floating with time and Ophelia out of my days.

Other Poems

WITNESSES

NOT snow
but snowdrops
clumped in corners
whitening river banks
or under bare trees,
fragile, stubborn,
braving winter out,
whatever else it defeats.

The small bunches
I give into your hand
silently each year
in Love's delicacy,
faded with the minutes,
though the memory of
their warm moment
lives on and on.

Not these new witnesses
I share with you now
at this quickening hour
where unchained, they drift
in great tides
before my glad eyes
milky and moist
beneath a drowned sky.

These are in infinity,
pure and untroubled,
as Love is,
yearly increasing
constant and beautiful,
as Love will.

Other Poems

NOTES

'The Bourgeois' (p31)

Typical of the sort of short Imagist-inspired piece found in *Poems* (1940), the reference to 'cowering hedges' may be a sub-conscious echoing of T.E. Hulme's famous poem 'Autumn' in which he saw the 'ruddy moon lean over a hedge'.

'After a Symphony by Glazunov' (p32)

Alexander Glazunov (1865-1936) was a Russian composer of the late Romantic period. In total he composed eight symphonies with sketches existing for a ninth. Although later incorporating more Western elements into his music, his first two symphonies are distinctly Russian in character, and it may have been these that Clark refers to here. The poem also pre-empts Clark's later habit of writing about places he had never visited, which he researched often quite thoroughly before imagining them in his mind.

'X' (p34)

Although not a portrait of a woman 'coiled in the wicker chair/beneath the yellow light' it is possible from the title that Clark was making a surreptitious reference to John Singer Sargent's painting *Madame X* (Metropolitan Museum of Art, New York). This iconic picture of Virginie Gautreau would seem to accord with last two lines of the poem: 'How insecure you are/for all your arrogance'.

'In Memoriam: Ivor Gurney' (p35)

First published in *The Gloucester Citizen*, 7 January 1938. As with F.W. Harvey, Clark was a great admirer of Gurney who was also a fellow poet of Gloucestershire. In the 1960s Clark was to collate and publish a selection of Gurney's verse and act as an important advocate for his work.

'Scaleber Beck' (p42)

Scaleber Beck is a natural beauty spot on the edge of the Yorkshire Dales, near Skipton. It is the location of Scaleber Force, an impressive 40-foot-high waterfall. Whilst visiting, Clark reputedly found the body of a drowned man and this recollection is fused in the poem with his own feelings of despair.

'Exiles' (p45)

The dedicatee of this poem, DJC, was Jane Callow, a teacher who Clark first met in Hereford in 1944 at a training course. They corresponded for a number of years before finally marrying in 1953. They were to have two children, Bob and Mary-Louise. The poem finds Clark reflecting on the breakdown of his first marriage and his burgeoning feelings for Jane.

'The Walk' (p60)

Edmund Blunden (1896-1974) was an English poet and critic. Clark first met Blunden in 1950 after the latter had returned from Japan where he had been part of the British liaison mission. Within his memoirs Clark describes the closeness of their friendship including visits to schools when Clark was an inspector as well as games of cricket with the family. Blunden's last publication was a *festschrift* to Walter de la Mare which he co-edited with Clark.

'English Morning' (p61)
Christopher Hassall (1912-1963) was an English poet, lyricist, and librettist who first became famous for his musical partnership with Ivor Novello. Hassall wrote the lyrics for six of Novello's popular musicals. Later he became a poet of great distinction winning the Hawthornden Prize for *Penthesperon* (1938). Clark first met Hassall whilst living in Leeds. Hassall contributed a book – an edition of the posthumous poems of the actor Stephen Haggard – to the Salamander Press, which Clark had recently founded with the publisher Edmund Arnold.

'Headlong, Like Comet' (p63)
Percy Wilson was a senior Inspector of Schools in the 1960s. He worked extensively with Leonard Clark who held him in high regard.

'The Clock' (p65)
The dedicatee of the poem is Iris Allam, wife of the composer Edward Allam with whom Clark lodged when he moved to Leeds. The clock had passed down through Iris's family, but she did not particularly like it and it did not go. Clark was told he could have the clock if he got it working. He got it repaired and took it with him when he moved to London in 1954. Martin Tupper (1810-1889) was a widely read novelist and poet of the Victorian period whose *Proverbial Philosophy* was a bestseller and who was even considered for the Laureateship following the death of Wordsworth. Today he is unread, and his books have been out of print for over a century.

'Far Headingley' (p71)
Headingley is a suburb of Leeds. The Allams' house, where Clark lodged while he lived in Leeds, was in Headingly, and as a lover of cricket he often visited the famous ground.

'Hedgehog' (p72)
Andrew Young (1885-1971) was a Scottish poet and clergyman. In 1941 he became Vicar of Stonegate in Sussex before being made a canon of Chichester Cathedral. Although rejecting much of his earlier work, his later style included a number of longer religious poems. He was a close friend to Clark who not only encouraged Young in his writing but who also made selections of his work and edited a critical appreciation.

'The Thief' (p73)
Henry Treece (1911-1966) was an English poet and writer who also worked as an editor and schoolteacher. Like Clark he wrote across a wide range of genres and became well known as an author of historical novels for children.

'Village Idiot' (p74)
First published in *The Inspectors' Bulletin*, April 1956.

'Wild Parsley' (p77)
Written on the island of Sark in 1954. This is where Leonard Clark and his second wife went on honeymoon.

'Button Box' (p80)
The box existed, and belonged to Sarah George, Clark's foster-mother in Cinderford.

'Samuel Palmer at Shoreham' (p82)
First published in *Prism: An Anglican Monthly*, February 1959 under the title 'West to East' the original version of the poem was slightly different to that later included in *Walking with Trees*. The later version is an improvement. In the second half of the 1960s Clark acquired a small reproduction of a Palmer drawing (a preliminary study for 'Pastoral Scene') and must have felt that the earlier poem (slightly modified) fitted perfectly with the image. Samuel Palmer (1805-1881) was a British landscape painter, etcher, and printmaker whose pastoral vision was a key continuation of Romanticism into the Victorian age. Inspired by William Blake, Palmer lived for nearly a decade in Shoreham, Kent where he associated with likeminded artists who became known as the Ancients. Clark found Palmer's work inspirational.

'Expression of Colour' (p83)
First published in *Prism: An Anglican Monthly*, February 1959.

'Boy and Grasses' (p84)
First published in *The Inspectors' Bulletin*, October 1960.

'Assembly of Birds' (p85)
The inspiration for this poem was a wall hanging given to Clark as a present by an educational official from China who he hosted as part of his work as an HMI of Schools. Clark was subsequently inspired to research the original painter, Huang-Chu'än (Huang Quan), one of whose pieces was an 'assembly of birds'.

'Bullfinches' (p86)
The bullfinches were seen in Clark's garden in Highgate. Carl Linnaeus (1707-1778) was a Swedish biologist who formalized the modern system of naming and classifying organisms. To this day scientists still use the Linnaean classification system.

'Every Voice' (p90)
Clark considered this to be his best poem. Between the early 1950s and 1980, this, the rest of *Singing in the Streets*, and some other poems, were privately printed as Christmas cards and sent by Clark to his family and friends.

'The Pea Pickers' (p105)

First published in *Words Etcetera*, Vol II, No I, 1973. The event happened, in the early 1960s. Clark had to travel to Peterborough for a Department of Education meeting and took his son Bob for the adventure. The poem was drafted on the return train journey. The poem includes a factual error – the signal did not drop in that location, rather, it rose for the train to go. But in his mind, Clark saw it drop to go, as it had in the Gloucestershire of his youth.

'Children of Islington' (p109)

On 1 April 1954, Clark joined the London Metropolitan Division of Her Majesty's Inspectorate of Schools, where he was to remain until his retirement. His area covered much of north London including Islington, and working with the London County Council he was to become very familiar with many of the local schools. He had this to say in his memoirs: 'I soon discovered that Islington had enormous problems, many of which I had never before encountered. The district, once a good residential area, had gone down a great deal since the war. Many of the middle-class families had moved farther out of London, and less well-off families moved into their houses. These houses, which had once accommodated single families, were now split up into flats and rooms. Much of this property was in poor condition, and badly needed repainting and additional sanitary provision' (Clark, 1976, 142).

'De La Mare's Bell' (p110)

Along with Andrew Young and Edmund Blunden, Walter de la Mare (1873-1956) was the strongest literary friendship in Clark's life. A chapter in *A Fool in the Forest* was devoted to recalling his meetings with de la Mare at his house in Twickenham: 'I know how this true and unswerving man accepted life and came to terms with it; I am still amazed by his ranging imagination, his endless questionings and experiments, his letters and kindnesses. If there is any celestial hall for poets, then surely a laurel-crowned easy chair (for how could *he* be comfortable on marble?) is already occupied by him' (Clark, 1965, 124). A few months before de la Mare's death, Clark visited him and took his baby son, Bob. The child was uninterested in the old poet but fascinated by the bell he kept on his bedside table to summon 'N', his nurse, and was the 'blithe bellman' of the poem. Subsequently, Clark claimed the bell for his son. Bob knew the story of the bell from early childhood, but as a teenager asked Clark to write it down, saying that no-one would ever believe him about the bell's story. Clark said he had already done so and produced this poem, first published in *New Poems 1960: A PEN Anthology* (Hutchinson, 1960).

'In Norfolk' (p112)

Inspired by a family holiday staying at Overstrand, Norfolk, in the mid-1960s. The poem notes the nearby samphire marshes, and a visit to the church at Knapton which has three tiers of angels in its hammer-beam roof.

'Fallow' (p114)

First published in the *Anglo-Welsh Review*, Winter 1972.

'IX' and 'XIX' (p115 and116)
These poems are drawn from a sequence of 22, put together into book form – *Silence of the Morning* – and limited to 100 copies. In the early 1970s Clark developed an intense cerebral fascination with JW, a young nurse, who, like him half a century earlier, had come from the West Country to work in London, and who unwittingly became his poetic muse. Many of Clark's poems concerned places he had never visited, but which attracted his interest, formed the subject of research, and which he then explored in his mind. The often-intense poems inspired by JW are comparable in that they recount imagined events and exchanges.

'Retreat to Silence' (p118)
From *12 Poems for St Bartholomew's*, a small pamphlet written to raise money for the church's upkeep and restoration. St Bartholomew the Great is located in Smithfield, City of London and was originally founded in 1123 by Rahere, a prebendary of St Paul's Cathedral, as an Augustinian priory. It was the local church for JW, and although he lived in Highgate, in the last years of his life, Clark (a committed high church Anglican), worshipped there regularly: his funeral service took place in the church in September 1981.

'Green Man Wandering' (p119)
Clark was proud of this poem and told his son Bob that it had been inspired by the poet Andrew Young. It was first published in *Aquarius No 1*, 1974.

'Cider-House' (p121)
Written for the Stroud Festival in 1974, and first published in the festival programme.

'Still Born' (p124)
First published in *Poetry Survey*, April 1977.

'Rector' (p127)
The subject of this poem is Prebendary Newell Wallbank, Rector of St Batholemew-the-Great, Smithfield, London, who Clark knew from the 1960s and who officiated at Clark's funeral service.

'Sermons in Stones' and 'The Way It Was' (p129 and p131)
Both JW-inspired poems. The first poetically describes reality, the second was dreamed.

'I', 'III', 'V', 'IX' and 'XII' (pp132, 134, 136, 137, 139)
An Intimate Landscape (1981) comprised 16 poems and was illustrated with wood engravings by Miriam Macgregor. It was limited to 500 copies and was written in 1979 and 1980 around the time of Clark's last visit to the Forest of Dean. Many of the poems are therefore nostalgic in tone. 'V' was first published in *The Countryman*, Winter 1979-80.

'XVIII' and 'XIX' (p141 and p142)

From *Winter to Winter*, a sequence of 30 poems again inspired by JW. Although intended to be published in 1978, a letter from the publishers dated 2 June 1978 indicates that a fire at the binders had destroyed all copies. Clark subsequently put a hold on publication considering that some of the poems should be revised but died before he had done so. The full sequence exists only in manuscript form.

'The Fortress' (p143)

One of twenty poems existing in manuscript which formed a sequence entitled *Burnt Siena* and detailing a trip made by Clark to that ancient city in Tuscany which caught Clark's attention and was the subject of research before an extended visit in his mind. Had he lived longer, *Burnt Siena* would have been Clark's next published book.

'When Snow Falls' (p144)

Published only in *For David Gascoyne on his 65th Birthday* (Enitharmon Press, 1981). Written for that book. Gascoyne had the year before written a poem for the *festschrift* commemorating Clark's 75th birthday.

'Silence and Water' (p145)

Published only in *Anglo-Welsh Review*, Winter, 1969.

'Witnesses' (p146)

Published only in *People Within* (anthology), Thornhill Press, 1973.

Works by Leonard Clark:

Between the Hills (1924, London: Arthur H. Stockwell)

Poems (1940, London: The Fortune Press)

Passage to the Pole and Other Poems (1944, London: The Fortune Press)

Rhandanim. Poem by Leonard Clark (1945, Leeds: The Salamander Press)

The Mirror and Other Poems (1948, London: Allan Wingate)

English Morning and Other Poems (1953, London: Hutchinson)

'Introduction' to *Andrew Young. Prospect of a Poet*, edited by Leonard Clark (1957, London: Rupert Hart-Davis), 11-21

Selected Poems, 1940-1957 (1957, London: Hutchinson)

Green Wood. A Gloucestershire Childhood (1962, London: Dennis Dobson)

A Fool in the Forest (1965, London: Dennis Dobson)

'Free Miners and Foresters' in *The Listener*, 22 September 1966, 422-423

Fields and Territories (1967, London: Turret Books)

Grateful Caliban (1968, London: Dennis Dobson)

Walking with Trees (1970, London: Enitharmon Press)

Secret as Toads (1972, London: Chatto & Windus)

Singing in the Streets. Poems for Christmas (1972, London: Dennis Dobson)

The Hearing Heart (1974, London: Enitharmon Press)

The Broad Atlantic (1975, London: Dennis Dobson)

The Inspector Remembers. Diary of One of Her Majesty's Inspectors of Schools, 1936-1970 (1976, London: Dennis Dobson)

Silence of the Morning (1978, Enitharmon Press)

The Way it Was (1980, London: Enitharmon Press)

An Intimate Landscape (1981, London: Nottingham Court Press)

As I Looked Over Jordan (1984, Kinnesswood: The Lomond Press)

Other works cited in the Introduction:

John Betjeman, 'Leonard Clark: A Memoir' in Leonard Clark, *As I Looked Over Jordan*

Jason Griffiths, *Reading the Forest: A history and analysis of Forest of Dean literature,* PhD thesis, University of Gloucestershire, 2019

Ian Hamilton (ed), *The Oxford Companion to Twentieth-Century Poetry* (1996, Oxford: Oxford University Press)

Keith Tuma (ed), *Anthology of Twentieth-Century British and Irish Poetry* (2001, New York: Oxford University Press)

TITLE INDEX

I 'A landscape of trees, massed ... ' *132*
III 'Almost no history ... ' *134*
V 'It was the warm smell of honeysuckle ... ' *136*
IX 'It was an orchard of plum trees ... ' *137*
IX 'Working on an old poem late at night ... ' *115*
XII 'When the nights drew in, they quietly came back ... ' *139*
XIX 'Iron man, speak to me ... ' *116*
XIX 'The land, a chessboard of brown squares ... ' *142*
XVIII 'I marvel at it ... ' *141*

Abyss *44*
After a Symphony by Glazunov *32*
Assembly of Birds *85*

Badger *87*
Bear *94*
Bees *93*
Biological Experiment *123*
Blackbird *39*
Bones *78*
Boy and Grasses *84*
Bullfinches *86*
Button Box *80*

Cave Painting *97*
Charcoal Burners *69*
Children of Islington *109*

Cider-House *121*
Clamavi *55*
Conceit *33*

De La Mare's Bell *110*

English County *104*
English Morning *61*
Every Voice *90*
Exiles *45*
Expression of Colour *83*
Eyes and Voices *107*

Fallow *114*
Far Headingley *71*

Grass *99*
Green Man Wandering *119*

Headlong, Like Comet *63*
Hedgehog *113*
Hedgehog *72*
Heron *53*
Hills *102*

In Memorium: Ivor Gurney *35*
In Norfolk *112*
Intensity *41*
Invasion *67*

January *81*
January Morning *56*
Journey Between Two Points *37*

Lamb *52*
Larks and Curlews *76*
Let These Things Be *58*
Looking at Cornfields *92*

Maurice *126*
Mole *103*
Mushrooms *88*
Mystical *46*

Near Tintern 1798 *68*

Peace, Like a Lamb *62*
Peaches *91*

Rector *127*
Retreat to Silence *118*

Samuel Palmer at Shoreham *82*
Scaleber Beck *42*
Sermons in Stones *129*
Silence and Water *145*
Small Life *101*
Still Born *124*

The Acorn *50*
The Bourgeois *31*
The Clock *65*
The Elements *89*
The Fortress *143*
The Hill *59*
The Lion *49*
The Mirror *47*
The Moth *36*
The Park *75*
The Pea-Pickers *105*
The Rocks *79*
The Seeker *57*
The Thief *73*
The Tower *48*
The Walk *60*
The Way it Was *131*
The Wilderness *51*

Victims *43*
Village Idiot *74*

When Snow Falls *144*
Wild Parsley *77*
Witnesses *146*

X *34*